Sukhmani Sahib
The Jewel of Peace

Sat Naam, Har Simrat
Kaur.

May the Light and
wisdom of the
Guru guide you
and protect you all
the days of your life.

With Divine Love,

Composed by
Guru Arjan

Translated by

Ek Ong Kaar Kaur Khalsa

Kaur Khalsa

Other published works by Ek Ong Kaar Kaur Khalsa:

Guru Nanak's *Japji Sahib: The Song of the Soul*
Guru Amar Das's *Anand Sahib: Song of Bliss*
Success and the Spirit: An Aquarian Path to Abundance from the Teachings of Yogi Bhajan

For additional translations of the writings of the Sikh Masters by
Ek Ong Kaar Kaur, please visit www.ekongkaark.com.

DEDICATION:

To the Radiant Presence of the fifth Sikh Master, Guru Arjan Dev ji—

You wrote the most beautiful, positive, and uplifting song about the potential of the human being. You created a vista of hope in a world where people had forgotten their greatness—and for that you were tortured. In the end, you proved the power of your words by smiling in the face of death.

Thank you for teaching us about the immensity of the human Spirit, the positivity of life, and the unconquerable nature of the Soul.

Special Thanks

No project is ever individual and nothing happens in isolation. This work has relied on the inspiration, support, and help of many people.

Thank you to my teacher Siri Singh Sahib Bhai Sahib Harbhajan Singh Khalsa Yogiji for chiseling and pushing me. Without your kind touch and encouragement, I would have never attempted to do any of these translations. Your faith in me and your guidance of the translation process has made my life richer than I can ever express.

Thank you to Dr. Balkar Singh, former head of the Siri Guru Granth Sahib Department at Punjabi University in Patiala, India. Your scholarly instructions over the years helped me create a context and understanding of Gurbani that has allowed these translations to mature and develop. I appreciate the philosophical conversations we have shared and the insights those discussions have given along the way.

I am so grateful to my family and friends who have supported me throughout the years, especially my late father, Jim Gillece, my mother Dee Gillece, my sister Michelle Martin, and my brothers Michael and James Gillece. Thank you to my friends Dev Suroop Kaur Khalsa, Sat Purkh Kaur Khalsa, Abhai Raj Singh, Inni Kaur Dhingra, Himat Kaur Khalsa, Dr. Japa Kaur Khalsa, Harpal Singh Khalsa, Dharmatma Kaur Khalsa, Jivan Joti Kaur Khalsa, Tera Kaur Khalsa, Har Nal Kaur Khalsa, Gurubhai Singh Khalsa and so many others. Thank you also to my two mentors from The KRI Aquarian Academy, Hari Charn Kaur Khalsa and Siri Neel Kaur Khalsa. Thanks especially to Sarb Nam Kaur Khalsa for her help with copyediting this manuscript.

I also want to give a special shout-out to my SikhNet family —for whom I am so very grateful. Guruka Singh Khalsa, Gurumustuk Singh Khalsa, Gurujot Singh Khalsa and Harijot Singh Khalsa, plus the entire SikhNet board - Supreet Singh Manchanda, Dr. Harjot Kaur Singh, Guru Amrit Singh Khalsa, Harbhajan Singh Khalsa, Guru Sevak Singh Khalsa and Panch Nishan Kaur Khalsa.. Thanks for giving me something wonderful to do for a living every day.

A profound thanks to those of you who helped financially support the production and printing of this translation. Especially Dr. Kirpal Singh.

Most importantly—thanks to all of you who have read these humble translations of the Sikh Masters that I have been blessed to do. Your feedback and incredible appreciation inspire me to keep up with this special work.

Through Guru Naanak, may Thy Spirit forever increase and may all people prosper by Thy grace. Naanak Naam, Charhdee Kalaa, Tayray Bhaanay Sarbatt Daa Bhalaa. Wahe Guru Ji Ka Khalsa, Wahe Guru Ji Ki Fateh.

Sardarni Sahiba Ek Ong Kaar Kaur Khalsa

Introduction

The fifth master in the Sikh tradition, Guru Arjan Dev ji, was born in Goindval, Punjab, India, and lived from 1563-1606. He became the fifth in a line of 10 Sikh Gurus in 1581. His life exemplified meditation and service. He made extraordinary contributions to the Sikh path during his time. Guru Arjan is notably remembered for two significant accomplishments.

Guru Arjan was a literary and musical genius. He composed over 2,000 original devotional songs, known as *Shabads*. He included these songs in a compilation called the *Adi Granth*. The *Adi Granth* included songs from the previous four Sikh masters—Guru Naanak (1469-1539), Guru Angad (1504-1552), Guru Amar Das (1479-1574), and Guru Ram Das (1534-1581), as well as songs from Hindu and Sufi saints.

The main teaching of the Sikh tradition is to see the One Divine Light in all Creation. The *Adi Granth* embodied this tenet of oneness by being the first truly inter-faith sacred work. It included the songs of wise people from diverse times and backgrounds whose poetry resonated with the Sikh Gurus' message of Oneness.

The creation of the *Adi Granth* signaled a key milestone in Sikh history. While working on the *Adi Granth*, Guru Arjan kept the sacred work on his bed while he slept on the floor. This act of devotion presaged what would happen during the time of the tenth Sikh master, Guru Gobind Singh (1666-1708). During his Guruship, Guru Gobind Singh incorporated the sacred writings of his father, Guru Teg Bahadur (1621-1675) into the *Adi Granth*. Guru Gobind Singh's creation of a second incarnation of the *Adi Granth* evolved into the *Siri Guru Granth Sahib*, which serves as the eternal living embodiment of Divine Wisdom for the Sikh community.

In the Sikh tradition, the Word is the Teacher and is the center of Sikh meditation, learning, and culture.

Another extraordinary act of devotion by Guru Arjan is that he allowed his body to be physically tortured in order to defend the integrity of the *Adi Granth*. Through political intrigue, Guru Arjan faced many accusations from Jahangir, the ruling Mughal Emperor of the time. When the Emperor decided to require Guru Arjan to pay a fine and ordered him to delete a number of "objectionable" verses from the *Adi Granth*, Guru Arjan Dev ji refused. The Emperor then demanded the Guru undergo a terrible, torturous punishment.

Guru Arjan was forced to sit on a metal plate that had a constant burning fire beneath it. Hot sand was poured over his body. This torture continued non-stop for five days and five nights.

When the Muslim saint, Mian Mir, asked Guru Arjan if he could do anything to stop the torture, Guru Arjan turned down the offer. Instead, the Guru showed Mian Mir a vision. In the vision, Mian Mir saw Guru Arjan stoking the fires under the hot plate, pouring the hot sand over his own body, and Guru Arjan himself overseeing his torture. Confused by the vision, Mian Mir asked for an explanation. Guru Arjan told him that everything happens by the Will of the One. And since the Guru did not feel separate from the Divine Will, there was no "other" involved in the torture at all. Guru Arjan smiled through the ordeal, proclaiming, "Thy Will is sweet to me."

After five days and nights, Guru Arjan requested to take a bath in a nearby river. By this point his body was completely blistered and burned. The prison guards agreed. They put Guru Arjan in a net and lowered him into the river. While under the water, Guru Arjan's body dissolved directly into the Light. The net was empty when the guards retrieved it. Through Guru Arjan's example of sacrifice, this extraordinary, Divine man left a legacy that would uplift humanity forever.

The composition in this translation—*Sukhmani Sahib (Jewel of Peace)*— is one of Guru Arjan's songs. It is the longest composition in the *Siri Guru Granth Sahib*, continuing for 36 pages or "limbs" of the Guru Granth.

It took more than eight years to complete this poetic interpretation. Meditating on *Sukhmani Sahib* in this way deeply changed my life.

Sukhmani Sahib is probably one of the most outrageously positive songs ever written about human consciousness and the human condition. In this modern world full of negativity delivered through a constant barrage of media, gossip, and news, where it sometimes seems that we do nothing but ferret out each other's weaknesses for cruel intentions —*Sukhmani Sahib* seems almost impossible to comprehend. In these verses, Guru Arjan unabashedly celebrates the uplifting relationship between the human and the Creator. He describes a life of potential Beauty possible for each one of us when such a relationship becomes the conscious center of our lives.

Many times during the translation process I was unable to digest what Guru Arjan wrote. I would stop and ask myself, "How can he say that? How can I possibly believe it?" The language was so overwhelmingly positive, so surrendered to a non-dualistic view of the Universe, and so carefree. His words challenged me to my core.

Slowly, over time, as the translation work continued, I found myself imbibing a little bit of that non-dualistic positivity and bliss. By allowing myself to align with the elevating vibration of *Sukhmani Sahib*, I found the strength and encouragement to walk through an extraordinarily challenging period in my life, doing my best to see it all as the play of the One.

Sukhmani Sahib represents a fractal of the Siri Guru Granth Sahib. It contains many of the main themes and messages that repeat throughout the 1,430 pages (traditionally called *Ang* or "limbs") of the *Siri Guru Granth Sahib*. The poetry of *Sukhmani Sahib* has tremendous depth and dimension. One can spend hours contemplating the meaning of just a few verses.

In *Sukhmani Sahib*, two themes are extremely powerful—the concepts of *Naam* and *Simran*. Understanding the meaning of *Naam* and *Simran* provides one of the main keys to appreciating this composition. Both terms carry complexity; like multi-faceted jewels, they sparkle and shine in different lines of verse within a unique context. *Naam* and *Simran* guide the way to helping us recognize our Divine, Infinite Identity in the midst of daily life.

In order to fully understand these two themes, I turned to the teachings of Siri Singh Sahib Bhai Sahib Harbhajan Singh Khalsa Yogiji (Chief Minister of Sikh Dharma of the Western Hemisphere), also known as Yogi Bhajan. The Siri Singh Sahib came to the West from India in the late 1960's, sharing the ancient science of Kundalini Yoga, and teaching about the Sikh Masters. He was my teacher and also my friend. That teaching and friendship continues to this day through his recorded lectures[1], even though the Siri Singh Sahib left his physical body on October 6, 2004.

This book contains two framing essays on the concepts of *Naam* and *Simran*. The essay on *Naam* comes from a talk I gave on November 1, 2014 where I incorporated quotes about *Naam* gleaned from various lectures by the Siri Singh Sahib. The essay about *Simran* is excerpted from a lecture by the Siri Singh Sahib on May 1, 1975. These insights from the Siri Singh Sahib about *Naam* and *Simran* helped guide my approach to this translation of Guru Arjan's *Sukhmani Sahib*.

Why are sacred works like this important? Because they give us a window to a different world. A world where human beings have completely activated their total potential by recognizing the Divine Light within themselves—a recognition that gives us each the opportunity to live truly happy, prosperous, and expansive lives.

Life is a gift. It does not last forever. Any moment that we can achieve true happiness – from the inside – without anything weighing us down – means we have embraced this gift and lived it to the fullest.

Sukhmani Sahib can take us to that place within ourselves where we see the One in all, and enjoy our lives in a care-free, loving and conscious way.

Translating *Sukhmani Sahib* was a humbling journey. Reading Guru Arjan Dev ji's words, there was no way to completely convey, in English, the depth, love, and unattached bliss of the original. By His grace, I have done the best job that I could – knowing that flaws exist.

---

[1]   www.libraryofteachings.com

However, if you appreciate this translation of *Sukhmani Sahib*, then find a recording in the original *Gurbani* and listen. It will transport you to a new dimension.

May you be blessed to live in the sovereignty of your own Divinity, and may your Light shine to heal, uplift and inspire all who meet you.

With Divine Light,

Ek Ong Kaar Kaur

What is Naam?

From a talk given by Ek Ong Kaar Kaur Khalsa on November 1, 2014.

The whole Sikh tradition centers on *Naam*. Gurbani talks about *Naam*. We read about *Naam* all the time. We hear about *Naam* in the stories of Sikh history. And the big mystery that everybody debates is: What is this *Naam*?

Naam is one of those terms in Gurbani that has different dimensionality based on the context as well as the point you are at in your own spiritual journey. Basically, you understand *Naam* from the perspective of your own consciousness, not based on an intellectual understanding of what *Naam* means.

When you look at the Siri Singh Sahib's teachings, he talks about *Naam* on many different levels. In the 1970s, he stayed with a very safe definition, "We chant the Holy *Naam*." In other words, we're just chanting God's Name. Then, in the 1980s and in the 1990s, as the community began to spiritually mature and have more experiences, he shifted the dialogue. He said, "Let me tell you what *Naam* really means."

The way he approached it when he taught in the West reflects the process students go through. *Naam* originally just means there is God's Name. Let me chant it. So I am going to chant *Raam* or I am going to chant *Har* or I am going to chant *Wahe Guru*. By reciting these words, I am doing *Naam japo*, (recitation of the Name) and that is what the Guru has asked me to do.

But when you taste what *Naam* gives you, the mind has an experience. That experience of *Naam* is what we want to explore.

There is a famous poem by T.S. Eliot called *The Naming of Cats*. In the poem, Eliot talks about the different names for a cat. And the last, most secret kind of name is the name that only the cat knows for himself through his own meditation. T.S. Eliot explains:

"But above and beyond there's still one name left over,
And that is the name that you never will guess;
The name that no human research can discover—
But THE CAT HIMSELF KNOWS, and will never confess.

"When you notice a cat in profound meditation,
The reason, I tell you, is always the same:
His mind is engaged in a rapt contemplation
Of the thought, of the thought, of the thought of his name:
His ineffable effable
Effanineffable
Deep and inscrutable singular Name."

When you get to that sense of what "ineffable name" means in T.S. Eliot's poem, that resonates with what *Naam* means in Gurbani.

In our spiritual practice, we chant the written, expressed names of the Divine. But the process of chanting awakens us to the *Naam*—which is an identity within each person that has no spoken equivalent. No one can understand the *Naam* except the *you* within you. According to the Siri Singh Sahib:

"Nobody understands that it is our primary, essential duty to recognize Naam. Naam is my identity given to me by my God complete and clear.

"This is all a Sikh has to learn—that, organically, God made you to learn. You need to learn to be you: not by process, not by group therapy, not by guidance. Learn to be you by reverence, by grace, by selflessness, and by self-esteem.

"There are a lot of people who want companions. It's not a bad idea. You should have a companion. Is your soul your companion? You are looking for a soul-mate. Are you looking for your soul? Are you looking for your Self? Are you identifying with your own identity?" (February 12, 1995)

Guru Nanak taught that your creative identity while you are living is a gift. It is something you need to recognize and deliver.

You are born with the seed of what you have a destiny to become, if that seed gets nurtured properly. In our spiritual practice, we chant *Har*. One way to talk about *Har* is as the Divine Seed or the Divine Essence.

Everyone is born with this Divine Seed. You are the Divine Light in form. You enter this time and space for an absolutely unique expression of creative reality that no other person can replicate. The talents you have and the circumstances you come into can turn into karma if you do not recognize your Identity. But if you train the mind to identify the *Naam* within you, then all of your experiences and all your talents can coalesce and flower into this unique You.

Sat Naam. Your Identity is what is authentic in you. What is authentic in you is your Divine Reality. Your authenticity is what you are here to express and realize. That becomes difficult if the mind gets trained to wear a mask and cast the fake self out into the world.

My favorite definition of *Naam* given by the Siri Singh Sahib is: "*Naam* is my identity given to me by my God complete and clear."

What he means is that you are a sovereign Identity. Nobody gets to tell you who you are. Nobody can know who you are. Only you can know who you are. No one else can know. It's my Identity that my Creator gave to me for a purpose.

"Guru Naanak is one man who gave Naam to the whole world. Naam has three conditions: Purkha, Prakriti, and Prakash. The ultimate being, the creative being and the light of the being. If that is mixed together in three words, it is called Naam. And Naam is Ek Ong Kaar. If somebody has to simro Naam then at least they should be wise enough to understand what they are talking about."— The Siri Singh Sahib (September 22, 1991)

Purkha, *Prakriti*, and *Prakash*: Every single one of us have these three qualities. *Purkha* is that stable, zero presence. We meditate and we get to the zero point where there is just stability, just presence. That is

Purkha. Prakriti refers to the creativity of the Divine. The movement, the transformation, the action, the flow. *Prakash* is the Divine Light at the core of our existence.

When we recognize and identify the *Naam,* that God-given Identity, it has these three qualities. I can be stable and present, powerfully creative and my Light shines through—all at the same time. If something takes you away from your stability and presence, then you cannot fully express the *Naam.* If something blocks you from your creative expression, then you cannot fully express the *Naam.* If something dims your Light, then you cannot fully express the *Naam.*

The challenge is that the mind exists, and the mind is a separate identity. The mind is the first servant of the soul, of the Inner Being, but it is not that Inner Being. The problem in the world is that humans have been shut off from the reality that they are Divine and that they have a Divine Identity. In that void, the mind becomes their identifiable identity. But the mind is not the Identity. It is a servant to the Identity. And when the servant takes over the house, a lot of problems result.

The process of *Simran* gives us a methodology to understand within ourselves what is the mind, versus what is *Naam.* How do I recognize my mental game or my ego or my shadow self, versus my authentic Being? How do I separate the fear that blocks me from fully expressing my *Naam* from the fearlessness that allows me to represent who I am in time and space?

That is the relationship between *Simran* and *Naam. Simran* gives you the doorway to understand what is mind and what is *Naam.* Mind is the servant. And *Naam* is the One who has to be served. This understanding becomes a great anchor. The mind must be trained. "Mind—you are not the Real Deal. You have to recognize and serve the Real Deal." This is how the ego surrenders. When the ego gets out of the way, then we can find this other taste within ourselves to rely upon that is Immortal.

The qualities of *Naam* that the mind has to recognize and understand are: *Purkha, Prakriti,* and *Prakash*—the stable presence, the creativity, and the Light all together.

When a person acts from those three forces combined, from a place of authenticity, he or she dwells in the *Naam*.

"To be a Sikh is to be objective to one's own personality. Naam. The very identity. A Sikh must not forget that he has an identity. Is he willing to sacrifice his identity to lie, cheat, deceive and abuse? Is it the character of a Sikh not to forgive? Is it the character of a Sikh not to share?

Karam is not a part of Sikhism. Karam is a part of the entire world. A Sikh is not bound by karam. A Sikh is bound by dharam. Dharam dominates in your actions.

Why can't we understand the simple things that Naanak said? 'Naam japo.' Purify your identity."—The Siri Singh Sahib (November 7, 1995)

When we first think about *Naam*, when we are starting off, we say, "I am just repeating the Name of God. *Har Har Har Har. Wahe Guru Wahe Guru Wahe Guru Wahe Guru. Sat Naam Sat Naam Sat Naam Sat Naam.*"

That is the first step. Then, if you continue, you are not just repeating. You are purifying your Identity. You purify yourself to express and identify the *Naam* within you. You are not calling on something external. You engage these sacred sounds to call on something within you. When you can see it within you, then you can start to see it in the entire world.

"That's why we get our name from the Guru. Bahadur Singh is Bahadur Singh. It means brave lion. Any act he does, which is not brave, is against his identity. Whether he likes to act or not, doesn't matter. Whether he argues about it, wants it or not, doesn't matter. It is not his choice. He has no choice. —The Siri Singh Sahib (November 7, 1995)

The ego wants to have a choice about who you are and what you want and what you are going to do with your life. But when you recognize the Identity given by the Divine, you have no choice. It's part of *hukam*—the Cosmic Plan. You have to surrender to it. It's what is already written.

Guru Naanak talks about this in the first Pauree of *Japji Sahib*:

ਹੁਕਮਿ ਰਜਾਈ ਚਲਣਾ ਨਾਨਕ ਲਿਖਿਆ ਨਾਲਿ

Hukam rajaaee chaln(.)aa Naanak likhiaa naal.

Surrender yourself and walk the way of Spirit's Will.
Naanak, be with what is already written.

*"Sat—truth. Truth is. What is Sat? What is Sat Naam? Truth is you are.
The only truth, the highest and lowest and smallest and left and right, the
communist, the democratic, the republican truth is that you are alive. That's
the only truth. Sat. You are alive. That's the truth. You are sick but still alive.
You are healthy. You are still alive. You are tall. You are still alive. You are
dying but still alive. That's the only truth. There is no more truth than this.*

*"Don't try to find it, either. To find truth is a pure waste of time. It is
absolutely an obnoxious attitude of a lunatic. It's not needed. Truth is.
Sat is. There are these two words: Sat Naam. We speak it. Truth is. You
are alive and Naam is—identify that you are alive. Then don't be mean.
Don't be cheap. Don't lie. Don't play games. Stop all that. Naam means
identify."—The Siri Singh Sahib (June 18, 1989)*

The Siri Singh Sahib gets back to this idea of confronting the game of the
mind, by just noticing that you are alive, no matter what your mind wants
to create around your existence: "Oh, I'm too short, or I'm too this or I'm
too that." The mind creates a lot of games.

The idea is that you exist. Identify that you have life. If you honor
your existence, why misbehave? Misbehavior disrespects your own
life force. Lying. Cheating. Running around. Doing these things means
that you have not identified that you are an existence that needs to be
honored and respected.

*"Why do we chant Wahe Guru? We say, God is great and the Guru is the
one who guided us to that greatness. That's exactly what it means. That
means we have to live it. Naam does not mean what I tell you and what
you hear. Naam means identify."—The Siri Singh Sahib (June 18, 1989)*

Here is another definition that the Siri Singh Sahib gives in many lectures:

"Naam means noun. Noun is the name of a person, place or thing. It is a totality. Identity is a totality. Identity is a reality. Sat means you are alive and identify."

We want to holistically understand it. *Naam* means to apprehend the totality of the Identity. To behold yourself as a total being. Nothing missing. All parts included. The total reality that you are is *Naam*.

Naam also allows us to see this reality in another person. In the tree. In the sun. In the totality of existence. The all-inclusiveness of it. To not disregard anything or dismiss anything or blind yourself to anything.

In *Naam*, we leave nothing out. It's not like you look at yourself and say, "God made me. And now I am going to fix it."

Yet, we do this. We look at ourselves and say, "Look at how the Creator made me. This is wrong, this is wrong, this is wrong. I am going to do this, this, this and this to fix it."

That's why many of us develop a spiritual practice. To fix what God made. It takes a lot of time, wisdom and maturity to say, "O, I am not supposed to fix anything. I just need to accept everything. And realize my Self."

Accept all the karma you've been through. Accept the sadness and the tragedies. Accept the blessings. Accept the gifts. Accept the totality of your reality, because that is the Identity the Creator gave you. Why reject it?

Look at these practices that Guru gives. For example, don't cut your hair. This instruction helps us accept ourselves as we are. My pain comes from my mind's game that something is wrong.

We want to confront the subconscious at the deepest level and proclaim: there is no imperfection in the creation that I am.

"When I was a commanding officer of the armed guards, one night I went on a surprise visit to check the post. I was equidistant when the guard pointed the rifle straight at my chest and said, 'Who is there?'

"And I had to identify myself. I said, 'Friend.'

"Watch this now. He said, 'Password.'

"The moment he said 'password,' I hesitated and stopped. The moment I hesitated and stopped, I heard the bolt going. It means the bullet came into the barrel of the gun from the chamber.

"I gave the secret password. I heard the bolt going back. It means the bullet was re-chambered.

"He said, 'Pass friend, all is okay.'

"That is all spirituality is about. That's all religion is about. That's all Dharma is about. That is all this planet earth is about. And that's all the search is about. You stand before death. Many speak of courage, speaking cannot give it. It is only in the face of death that we live it. You speak before death and you say, 'I identify, God, that I am yours.' You know what God is going to say? 'Pass friend, all is okay.' If you have not learned that my dear friend, God knows where you are going to go."—The Siri Singh Sahib (June 18, 1989)

Simran and Seva

From a lecture given by Siri Singh Sahib Bhai Sahib
Harbhajan Singh Khalsa Yogiji on May 1, 1975.

Honest is honest. Dishonest is dishonest. But nobody has the right to judge it because somebody's judgment may be dishonest or honest. Why don't we judge? Because we cannot consolidate the total facts. This is one of the greatest miracles of life. No man has been given the capacity by the Creator to judge anybody because nobody has the virtue to know the total facts. Now, the beauty of the whole thing is, when we don't have all the facts, what can we do? We can only direct. We can't judge. We can judge in the light of direction...

If we judge to direct each other, it means we judge, we find a mistake and we help the person to come out of the mistake. If each one starts helping each other come out of the mistakes, where will the mistake be? If a mistake has been found in A, then B should say, "Oh, I have found the mistake! Now, let us work together to get out of it." Then there is no mistake. But if A says, "Oh, I have found the mistake, and I'm going to dump you with it," it becomes a harassment of life.

The biggest gift to a person is to find himself or herself or itself. A being must find his being-ness... If we will not find ourselves and practice how to sustain ourselves through all the pressures, then there will be nothing to sustain anything. Therefore, our faith within ourselves should be a tested faith.

The greatest beauty in the science of yoga is how the mind works. The mind works in one way. The intellect gives you a thought, and you run after the thought wave, or you stop. Every thought which comes to you through the thought wave, you stop and think about what you are thinking in the thought wave. If you correct the channel of the thought wave, you will never be in trouble in life. Don't correct yourself. Don't correct your ethics, your morals, your "yes" or your "no." Don't correct your polarity or your non-polarity. If you ever have to correct something, correct the thought wave.

All yogas will teach you to think to the root of the thought, thus eliminating the thought in deep meditation. Now, eliminating the thought in deep meditation may be a process, but it is not THE process. THE process is to correct the thought wave. That is why Guru Nanaak gave the power of *Simran*... *Simran* is meditation in the form to correct the thought form.

The science of *Simran* has not been talked about on this earth. It was maintained as a mystery even today. It has not been taught to humanity in public. It has always been person to person... We are talking about that secret science tonight, because we have to find the Oneness of the basis. People think repetition of a *Naam* is *Simran* or that the Guru gives a mantra and that is *Simran*. All these directions will work a bit. But they will not work out totally...

The power of *Simran*, the power of the syllable of the holy word, is actually the science of correcting the thought wavelength of the individual psyche. It's a complete and total science and it is a root science of yoga. Without this science, which has been kept as a mystery, the science of yoga is not complete. That is why there are millions of yogis, but nobody knows what yoga is... This is the learning. The thought wave has to be corrected so that the intellect can send the correct thought wave. This way, the entire energy of a person will not be used in correcting himself or herself all the time. That's what we are going to discuss today. Patience pays.

You have an obligation to your You. Within you, you have a You and that You demands that you must provide the experience to that You within you. Without that experience, that You is not satisfied. You promise that You every day, "My You, just hold on. Tomorrow, I'm going to hook somebody. I'm going to provide You this. I am going to do this for You." You continuously talk to your own You all the time. It is an unstopping vicious circle. Each day, you talk to your You. Each day, you communicate, you receive direction, you flirt with it, you lie to it and each day, you know that you are not doing the right thing. Each day, you are promising your own You. But each day, you are cheating your own You. Then you come out before the world and you say you are a very honest person.

It is fascinating that we don't have the wisdom to see how we function. This is Maya. Nobody knows that each one talks to his very self. Each one directs himself. Each one receives direction for himself…

"I am worried." What is the worry? Worry is nothing but a conflict between you and You. "I doubt very much." You doubt very much because there is a tremendous split between you and your You. When you deny that you have a You within you, you deny a lot of things to yourself. That's why your scene is never together because you are never together with your own You.

Science has told you that you have a subconscious. Your subconscious You is the You within you. It talks to you. It speaks to you. It suggests things to you. It receives some satisfaction from you. It takes a new promise from you every day. You are ethically, morally, by experience and by virtue of existence feeding your subconscious every moment and you do it voluntarily.

That is where Naanak came with the greatest science of the world. He said, in feeding the subconscious, change the direction. He introduced the greatest mystical science of *Simran*.

People said to him, "We will do *Simran*. We love to find ourselves. We love to experience ourselves. We love to change our thought pattern by changing our thought direction. O, Guru, You are the greatest being. You teach us how to super-master our intellect."

That is what manners are, to master yourself with the intellect, which is the fountain of the thought source. As much mastery as you have on your intellect, that much intelligence you have…

The structure of Sikh Dharma is based on two pillars: *Simran* and *seva*.

Seva is service. You can win everybody with *seva*. There is a beautiful story.

There was a little kingdom in the foothills of the Himalayas. It was a very precise community. The adjoining king became greedy and attacked. People with great bravery fought, but they lost the war. When the victorious force came in, the people of the country, who lost the war, showed such a discipline, such a training of mind and gave them such help to establish themselves, the enemy forgot that they are the victorious army. Instead, they thought that they are the guest armies coming to another country.

Instead of declaring the king to be the subject of the other king, they both met like brothers and a friendship was established. It is one record in human history available for all of us that good manners serve you even in defeat.

Good manners are good everywhere. Good personalities are good everywhere. Goodness is good everywhere. How can one achieve goodness? That is the science of *Simran*. Arising consciousness through the chakras, through the ultimate chakra. It is the science of Kundalini, and it is exactly the science of *Simran*.

What is the process of life? The process of life is commitment and experience. *Simran* and *seva*. Nobody can correct the state of mind without making the mind to commit or making the mind to experience.[2]

… Ninety percent of people are mentally sick because they don't have the satisfaction they have committed. Ninety percent. When you do not have the satisfaction and experience that you have committed, you will sidetrack your life. You will not be guiding your life under the very You. The supremacy of the outer you has to direct the inner You. So the mind cannot be allowed to master the intellect. Therefore, the experience of commitment is the highest experience.

---

[2]   The previous five paragraphs originally were spoken by Yogi Bhajan earlier in the lecture. However, an editorial decision was made to move this section for the sake of readability and flow.

You do *Simran*. What will *Simran* do? *Simran* will raise your consciousness. *Charhdee Kalaa*. Kundalini and consciousness are not two things. It's the name of the same game. One is ancient and one is new, that's all. *Simran* will raise you to be more aware. It will widen your horizon. You will see better. You will see more. And what will you do then? Then you will serve and that is s*eva*...

We use the expression, "it is." It in itself is. It means the existence in time. So "it is" and "is it." ...Who recognizes the it? The outer being. Who recognizes the is? The inner being. So we have two beings within ourselves...

The first action of *Simran* is: you have to recognize that you have a complex You. That's the first expansion. Second is, without your knowledge, your inner You has a constant thought wave. With you, your inner self has the right to exchange the thought wave.

Therefore, you must administer your outer you to challenge that authority of complete sovereignty of the inner You; and you must make the inner You look to and compromise with the outer you; and the outer you must compromise with the inner You so that you can carry on. Do you understand how you distinguish your expression of self in two times?...

There is tremendous evidence available that each person has a set personality. We call it personality in destiny. And the outer shell of that personality is noted down as the personality in time. So we have to deal with two personalities. This personality in destiny and personality in time. If the personality in destiny within the personality of time is delivered to the destiny, one has achieved liberation. If it is not done, then it is a continuous cycle of time, of come and go, come and go, come and go. We call it *aava-gavan*.

The theory of *aava-gavan* is that the soul has to reach a destination. Because it has already started, it must end. It started from Infinity, it must end in Infinity. One must have an experience to get into Infinity, into the oneness of God. To get into the oneness with God, a person has to learn to be one. One is only that one whose inner self and outer self experience the same thing at the same moment for the same oneness; of the cause-being-effect into the altitude and latitude of the personality in action and reaction both.

You know, I have to explain because this is the theory. It is impossible that the experience of action and reaction could both be the same. Impossible. Action has a reaction. How can the experience be the same?

You have to be above action and reaction. That is the *thuriya* stage. And *thuriya* stage can only be received in experience through the power of *Simran*. Within your action and within your action to reaction there is somebody supervising. If that supervisor is alert, he knows the action, the reaction, and also the direction. When action, reaction. and direction is known, the destiny is reached.

Each function has its pilot; whereas, the intellect is the pilot of your inner self, the intelligence is the pilot of your outer self. Who should have the control? The outer self. Because the outer self is what you represent to the world. The inner self is what you are.

What you represent to the world is what the world sees, not what you are. You think that what you are is what people see. But that's not true. You constantly show the world what you are but actually you are not that. If you represent consciously to the world what you want to represent, then you have a representation to the world.

What is ignorance and what is awareness? Awareness is when you represent what you want to represent. This is a jute mill. It is a mill, but what does it do? It produces jute. This is a rubber mill. What does it do? It produces rubber. He is a yogi, he produces yoga. He is a *bhogi*, he produces *bhoga*. He is a saint, he produces sainthood. He is a thief because he has a mastery of thievery. The mill is known by the production and man is known by his action.

Who governs the action?

Commitment.

Commitment is nothing but the action of the inner self to support the outer self. Commitment is not to give something to anybody. Commitment is when the inner self promises under certain longitude and latitude to support the outside of your own self.

Watch this expression. You are right. You are absolutely right. You are absolutely true, but I am committed to it. Commitment surpasses truth. Because commitment is truth. Achievement is the experience of your own commitment. In this life, you have no experience. Your experience is the experience of your commitment… because the inside and outside are both combined in that.

What is sorrow? Your inside and outside are separate in an action. Therefore unity of the being is unity of the inside and outside. Disunity is disunity between the being of inside and outside. What is *Simran*? *Simran* is the direction of the outside to the inside, to go into the deepest of the inside, to trigger the very inside, so the entire outside may correspond.

The science of *Simran* is nothing but to have immense power of *seva*. Service. Through service, you win the world. There is no other way known to man…

The only power of a human being on the other human being is how much one can serve the other. And what is a service? Tolerance towards direction of gainful profit. So it's a business.

You have to tolerate the other man's nuisance and direct him with your energy, so that the person may gain. If a person will gain, he will feel happy. When he feels happy, he will confide in you. When he confides in you, he will work according to you. He will work more, then he will gain more. He will gain more, then he will work more. Until he dies gaining everything he wanted. If he gains what he wanted to gain ultimately, then he is a gainful being. His ultimate gain is that he goes into the infinity of the gain and that is God. You gain through service.

The human mind can change the thought direction with the power of *Simran*. Where can we find a specific procedure, well established and qualified, where the power of *Simran* can be seen? It was an experiment in the spiritual world. Ten men of God came.[3] They tried to start with men who were the most rejected, self-depressed and totally self-condemned people. These men of God started processing them through the process of the *Simran*.

The more they were in the process of *Simran*, the more *Sat* (Truth) they found. The more *Sat* they found, the more *satya* came to them. Energy. Kundalini energy means *satya*. Power of the *Sat* is *satya*. The more power came, the more they did *Simran*. The more they found, the more they gave. The more they gave, the more they found. And thus from self-condemned people, they became self-alighted, self-delighted, self-inspired, and self-saints.

Then, they became soldiers. They became the protectors of sainthood. Actually, the Khalsa is a human in action for the protection of sainthood. And he protects through action. That is why their master, Guru Gobind Singh, gave them the family name, Khalsa. Why was this family name given? So that the very effect of it may remind a person. Remind which person? The inner self. The outer self lives it.

Now what is a thought pattern? A thought pattern is a *shabad*—the Word.

"In the beginning there was a Word. The Word was with God and the Word was God." [Ed. Note: Yogi Bhajan paraphrases *John 1:1* from the Bible.]

It's the thought pattern, the *shabad*. A combination from which the thought pattern can be changed is mantra... And what is a mantra? A mantra is a finite direction in existence towards Infinity through the thought pattern. That's why the mantra given to a person is *Wahe Guru*. *Guru* is the state of experience through a spiritual technology to direct the thought pattern. And *Wahe*—wow! How great is that pattern! It is the acknowledgement and it's a statement of experience.

---

[3] Yogi Bhajan is referring to the 10 Sikh Masters—Guru Naanak (1469-1539), Guru Angad (1504-1552), Guru Amar Das (1479-1574), Guru Ram Das (1534-1581), Guru Arjan (1563-1606), Guru Hargobind (1595-1644), Guru Har Rai (1630-1661), Guru Har Krishan (1656-1664), Guru Teg Bahadur (1621-1675), and Guru Gobind Singh (1666-1708).

If you look at this whole mystery—open it up and finalize it—when you find the result of it, you will be surprised to see it is a simple science of humanology, where years of an experiment have been made to prove how a man can conquer his fear and become fearless so that he can meet the Fearless.

You have to become fearless to meet the Fearless. You have to become great to meet the Great. You have to become infinite to meet the Infinite. You have to become beyond time and space to meet the One who is beyond time and space…

You work it any way, you will find out each man has to commit. The experience of commitment is to honor the commitment. And to honor the commitment is the act of the honorable. Guru Naanak vouched for it.

ਜਿਨੀ ਨਾਮੁ ਧਿਆਇਆ

Jinee naam dhi-aa-i-aa

Those who committed to meditate on the Naam,

ਗਏ ਮਸਕਤਿ ਘਾਲਿ ॥

Ga-ay masakat ghaal

And they did this hard job,

ਨਾਨਕ ਤੇ ਮੁਖ ਉਜਲੇ

Naanak tay mukh ujalay

He certifies it—they are with radiant face.

ਕੇਤੀ ਛੁਟੀ ਨਾਲਿ ॥੧॥

Kaytee chhut(.)ee naal

All their karmas have gone with them.—*Guru Naanak* (Shalok of *Japji Sahib*)

You can't know yourself without a mirror. The mirror of awareness is the law of happiness.

Simran Pranayam

(Kundalini Meditation as taught by Yogi Bhajan®)

Sa-Ta-Na-Ma is the Panj Shabad. They are the five primal sounds that when meditated upon bring the five elements into balance and open up one's sensitivity and awareness.

Inhale completely in 15 quick, short sniffs, mentally chanting *"Sa"* with each sniff, for a total of 15 times. Suspend the breath for one silent beat before going to the next part, for a total of 16 beats.

Exhale completely in 15 quick, short segments, mentally chanting *"Ta"* with each segment, for a total of 15 times. Suspend the breath out for one silent beat before going to the next part, for a total of 16 beats.

Inhale completely in 15 quick, short sniffs, mentally chanting *"Na"* with each sniff, for a total of 15 times. Suspend the breath for one silent beat before going to the next part, for a total of 16 beats.

Exhale completely in 15 quick, short segments, mentally chanting *"Ma"* with each segment, for a total of 15 times. Suspend the breath in for one silent beat before going to the next part, for a total of 16 beats.

Begin with 3 minutes. Add 1 minute per session and build up to 31 minutes.

What Yogi Bhajan said about this meditation:

"This is the *Simran Pranayam,* in which you have the authority to expand your consciousness, your ability, and your brain self. You can start making a hole in the five sections of the brain—right side and left side—so that the central brain can look equally over all.

"[Take]15 strokes in. It is the 16th breath, known as pranayam. Start with a maximum of three minutes and add one minute to it. [Work up to] 31 minutes, but there should be somebody standing by you in case you faint. If you faint, water should immediately be served."

Sukhmani Sahib

Ek Ong Kaar Sat Gurprasaad

One Spirit Beyond
Moves within
The Creation—
Coordinating
Consolidating
Continually
Creating.

This understanding
Shall come to you
As a blessing
As a gift
Through the Sound of Wisdom
That takes you to Truth.

1

Shalok

From the very start of time and space
There's been a Guiding Voice
Bringing us to Light.

O Guiding Voice,
To You I bow.

And as the stages and the ages
Of the Universe unfold,
That Guiding Voice
Continues on.

O Guiding Voice
To You I bow.

That Guiding Voice delivers me
To what is genuine and real—authenticity.

O Authentic Guide
To You I bow.

It is invisible and transparent
Ever present in the Unseen dimensions.

O Unseen Guide, unlimited in reach,
To You I bow.

1

Ashtapadi

1-1

When Spirit and my mind talk to each other,
And keep talking and talking
Until they come to a one-pointed understanding,
Only then do I find peace.

Through such an understanding,
All the pain, sickness and trouble held within my body
Completely disappears.

The Light of my mind penetrates through
To connect with the One who protects the Universe.

Countless beings are engaged in deep contemplation
On the Identity of the Divine.

The description of the sacred reality
Found in the writings of the sages

Comes from one single letter
Of the Divine Name.

For the person who lives
With the tiniest bit of that knowledge

Endless is his honor.
Countless are his praises.

There is only one thing I need—
To behold You, Divine One.

In the company of those
Who also long for Your sight

Naanak finds his liberation.

1-2

This sacred song of *Sukhmani,*
Which crystallizes the mind
Into a jewel of peace,

Brings comfort,
A sense of well-being
The realization of one's
Immortal, Divine nature,
And a connection to the Creator.

This song rests and relaxes
The minds of those
Who live in devotion to Thee.

(Pay attention)

Communicating with the Creator,
You won't come to dwell in the womb.

Communicating with the Creator,
The pain of death runs away.

Communicating with the Creator,
Death forsakes you.

By communicating with the Creator,
All enemies yield to you.

The very act of communicating with the Creator
Keeps obstacles from blocking you.

Communicating with the Creator,
You remain alert, day and night.

Communicating with the Creator
Fear ceases to exist.

Communicating with the Creator
Ends sorrow and suffering.

Keep company with those who live a pure life,
And communicate with the Creator.

Naanak, you will find the hue
Of the Divine Reality in you
And shall obtain all the treasures.

1-3

Communicating with the Creator
Brings wealth, reputation, mystical powers and the nine treasures.

Communicating with the Creator
Delivers wisdom, meditation,
Subtle understanding, and an experience of the Essence.

Communicating with the Creator,
Bestows the virtues of devotional recitation,
Inner purification,
And the offering of sacred gifts.

Communicating with the Creator destroys duality.

Communicating with the Creator is the cleansing bath.

Communicating with the Creator brings honor
In the Royal Court of the Divine.

Communicating with the Creator
Whatever happens is good.

Communicating with the Creator brings fulfillment and success.

The ones who communicate with You,
O Divine One,
Are those whom You inspire to do so.

Naanak clings to those who live like this.

1-4

Communicating with the Creator
Gives the most exalted experience.

By communicating with the Creator
So many find liberation.

Communicating with the Creator
Satisfies one's thirst.

Communicating with the Creator
One comes to understand everything.

Communicating with the Creator
There is no fear of death.

Communicating with the Creator
Fulfills one's desires.

Communicating with the Creator
Clears the darkness and dirt in the mind,

And causes a person
To merge into the Immortal Identity
Found in her heart.

The power of the Creator resides on the tongue
Of such a wise and saintly one.

Naanak serves those who serve Thee.

1-5

The one who communicates with the Creator
Has all his needs provided for.

The one who communicates with the Creator
Lives with prestige and honor.

The one who communicates with the Creator
Becomes an acceptable servant.

The one who communicates with the Creator
Is chief among men.

The one who communicates with the Creator
Lives in her sovereignty.

The one who communicates with the Creator
Commands everything.

The one who communicates with the Creator
Dwells in peace.

The one who communicates with the Creator
Is forever indestructible.

When Your kindness prevails,
O Creative Consciousness,
People embrace
Their inner dialogue with You.

Naanak seeks the dust of those who live this way.

1-6

The one who communicates with the Creator
Kindly gives to all.

May I surrender myself to forever serve and protect
Those who communicate with the Creator.

The one who communicates with the Creator,
His face glows with beauty.

The one who communicates with the Creator
Lives content and happy.

The one who communicates with the Creator
Experiences the victory of the soul.

The one who communicates with the Creator
Empties herself of everything but her purity.

The one who communicates with the Creator
Enjoys abundant ecstasy.

The one who communicates with the Creator
Feels cozy towards the Divine.

Through the kindness of those who live a pure life,
A person remains aware, all day and all night.

Naanak, when the destiny is perfected,
The mind and soul connect to establish a dialogue
That reaches Infinity.

1-7

Communicating with the Creator
All your work gets accomplished.

Communicating with the Creator,
There's nothing to worry about.

Communicate with the Creator
And vibrate the virtues of the Divine Reality.

Communicate with the Creator
And merge into the flow of life.

Communicating with the Creator
Makes you steady and strong
In the posture of your being.

Communicating with the Creator,
The lotus of awakening blooms.

Communicating with the Creator,
The Sound Beyond Sound rings and chimes.

The peace that comes from communicating with the Creator
Has no end.

When the Creative Consciousness moves with compassion,
Then someone practices this art
Of establishing a dialogue between the soul, the mind and Infinity.

O Naanak, go and find the protection of people like this.

1-8

Communicating with the Divine Reality,
Devotion becomes visible.

Communicating with the Divine Reality,
The record of sacred wisdom took form.

Communicating with the Divine Reality,
People spiritually awaken,
Restrain themselves in purity,
And become great givers.

By communicating with the Divine Reality,
The weak and lowly gain fame across the world.

Communicating with the Divine Reality,
The earth keeps moving along.

Let mind and Spirit
Spirit and mind
Keep speaking with each other

For it is the Creativity of Divinity
Who does all the deeds.

All forms came about through Simran

Through the Creator's decision
To have a dialogue with Itself
Through a finite voice with Infinite reach.

Communicating with the Divine Reality
Sense the Formless One within your own existence.

When Your kindness prevails, O Divine One,
We understand these things within ourselves.

Naanak, those who live by the Sound of Wisdom,
Learn to communicate with Infinity.

2

Shalok

O You who break the grip
Of poverty, sickness and pain,

Master of all these abandoned hearts,

Naanak comes to live with You
And take shelter under Your protection.

2

Ashtapadi

2-1

When there's no love from your mother or father,
No love from your children or friends,

In that moment, let your mind
Recognize the identity the Divine gave you.

This will be your companion and help you.

When the Angel of Death, terrible and frightening,
Comes to destroy you,

Only the identity which the Divine gave you
Will be with you when you go.

When difficulties wear you down
With their heavy weight and burden,

Recognize the Divine Reality
In every identity (including your own).
This will free you in an instant.

You can make amends so many times,
But that won't cross you over the ocean of life.

Recognize the Divine Reality
In every identity (including your own).

Then, the pain you feel over the million mistakes
Your ego has made will depart.

Mind of mine
Follow and surrender to
The instructions of the Teacher, the Guru.

And repeatedly call upon the *Naam*
The name of the One
That awakens the Divinely-Given Identity of a person.

O Naanak, then you will find peace in abundance.

2-2

One who rules over the entire world
Still feels misery and pain.

Happiness happens by chanting *Har*,
And calling upon one's Divine Identity.

Wealth that measures into the billions
Won't remove the obstacles that limit a man.

Freedom comes by chanting *Har*,
And calling upon one's Divine Identity.

There are countless pleasures in the earthly realm,
But none of them quench that thirst.

To be satisfied, chant *Har*
And call upon your Divine Identity.

When you come to a road that you must walk alone,
Recognize the Divine Reality
In every identity (including your own).

This will keep you company and bring you ease.

Such is the identity given to me by the Divine.
Mind, meditate upon it always.

Naanak, when you become wise
By living in tune with the Sound of Wisdom,
You shall achieve the highest status.

2-3

When billions of hands cannot help you escape,
Call upon the identity the Divine gave you.

You shall reach the other side.

When numerous shadows come to destroy you
Recognize the Divine Reality
In every identity (including your own).

It will save you in an instant.

As long as you are born through the womb,
Constantly dying and coming back again,

Call upon the identity the Divine gave you.
This shall bring you ease and peace.

The ego creates so much filth and dirt
That never gets cleared away.

Recognize the Divine Reality
In every identity, including your own.

It will remove the refuse of a million mistakes.

When you call upon your Divinely-given Identity,
Then your mind assumes Its color and hue.

Naanak, this experience will come to you
In the company of those who live by purity, grace and discipline.

2-4

On the road where you cannot know
How far you have left to travel,

The Divine Reality in every identity
Will provide for you and keep you company.

And should you encounter on your path
A massive darkness that blinds you,

The Divine Reality in every identity
Will stay with you and light your way.

If you recognize no one during your journey,

The Divine Reality in every Identity
Will be with you and understand.

When you suffer and burn under the glare and the heat,

The Divine Reality, through Its identity,
Will be there above you, giving you shade.

When your mind becomes distracted
By its own desires and thirsts,

Then, Naanak, let the continual presence
Of the Divine Essence
Activate the memory of your own Immortality

And let that nectar rain down.

2-5

Devoted lovers align their actions
With the identity the Divine gave them.

People of wisdom nurture and relax their own minds.

The Divine Reality, through Its identity,
Protects those who serve.

The Divine Reality, through Its identity,
Frees millions.

Those who live a pure life
Enjoy the sweet taste of that Divine Reality
Day and night.

Such people of wisdom
Have earned the healing medicine
That comes from being with the Divine constantly.

For those who live in service to the Divine Reality,

Experiencing that Sacredness
In themselves and all things
Is the treasure.

The Master gives this gift
To His servants.

Their minds and bodies absorb and become
The same color as the One.

O Naanak, such servants intuitively have discriminating insight.

2-6

Recognizing the Divine Reality in oneself and in all,
Is the method for people to become liberated.

Recognizing the Divine Reality in oneself and in all,
People feel full and satisfied.

Those who serve take on the form and color
Of their Divinely-given Identity.

Chant the name *Har*,
And call upon your Divine Identity.

It will keep things from falling apart.

Recognizing the Divine Reality in oneself and in all,
Makes people fantastic and great.

Recognizing the Divine Reality in oneself and in all,
People become beautiful.

Spiritual union and earthly pleasures
Come to those servants who
Recognize their Divine Identity.

Chant the name *Har*.

You will never feel separate from anything.

There are those who love to serve
The Divine Reality in every identity.

Naanak worships
The transparent, ever present consciousness
Of the continually Creative Divine One.

2-7

The unfolding of the Divine Potential,
Cosmic, creative, and continuous,
Is the wealth and treasure of those who serve Thee.

Master—You, Yourself, give Your servants the prosperous blessing
Of experiencing this Unfolding.

The unfolding of the Divine Potential,
Cosmic, creative and continuous,

Powerfully protects Your servants.

They know nothing but the light and radiance
Of that Creative Divine Consciousness.

Every fiber of the one who serves this Divine Unfolding
Is completely absorbed in the taste of it.

Immersed in total concentration at the zero point,
Merged with the still, clear awareness
At the heart of the Creative Play,

One becomes drunk on the taste
Of one's Divinely-given Identity.

Twenty-four hours a day,
Your servants chant

Har...Har...

Flowing with the continual unfolding
Of the cosmic, Divine Creativity.

Those who love this experience
Reveal themselves and do not hide.

By loving the unfolding of the Divine Potential,
So many become liberated.

O Naanak, scores of people swim across
By becoming the companions of Thy servants.

2-8

Recognizing the Divine Reality in oneself and in all
Will satisfy one's desires.

Singing in a sacred way
About the Unfolding of the Divine Potential
Will bring a person all they need.

Talking about the creative Divine Consciousness
Is the highest thing to do.

Deeply listening to one's Divine Identity
Ends pain, suffering and sorrow.

In the heart of those who live a pure life
Lives the grandeur of the Divine Self.

All one's ugly mis-steps run away
By being in the radiant presence
Of those who are wise and kind.

By tremendous good fortune, a person becomes
The companion of those who live purely.

Serving those who are wise
A person meditates on their Divinely-given Identity.

Nothing equals the Identity
The Divine gave you.

Naanak, some of those who live in tune with the Sound of Wisdom
Obtain their Infinite Self.

3
Shalok

I have searched through so many sacred texts
From so many religious traditions.

Worshipping something isn't the same as
Experiencing the Divine Reality
Or watching as It expands into Creative Expression.

O Naanak,
Knowing one's Divinely-given Identity
Is invaluable.

3
Ashtapadi

3-1

The repetition of sacred words and sounds,
Generating the inner fire to purify oneself,
Wisdom and knowledge,
All forms of meditation;

The explanation of sacred scriptures,
Yogic practices,
Doing one's duty,
Having a spiritual discipline,
Performing rituals;

Abandoning everything and wandering in the forest,
Making numerous efforts in so many different ways,
Giving an abundance of jewels as an offering,
Being attached to sacrificing the body by cutting it into pieces,
So many methods of fasting and practicing self-restraint;

None of these are equal to understanding,
Within your own consciousness,
The Identity of the One who created the dance
Between the sun and the moon.

Even if, O Naanak,
That Identity is called upon
Just once
By those who live in tune with the Sound of Wisdom.

3-2

A person can travel across
The nine continents of the earth
And live a full life,
Become a great renunciate and practice self-mortification,
Sacrifice his body in the fire,
Give gifts of gold, land and a variety of horses,
Hold many different yogic postures
And perform the rituals of inner-cleansing;

Allow pieces of the body to be cut
At any time,
In any moment;

Yet, with all this,
The subconscious filth of the ego
Doesn't depart.

Nothing equals
Experiencing the Divine Reality in every identity.

Naanak,
By living in tune with the Sound of Wisdom,
One attains the state of consciousness
Where she calls upon her Divine Self.

3-3

A person dips his body in sacred waters
To free the mind of its desires,

But the mind never wearies
Of its arrogance and its pride.

Even by bathing all day and all night,
The darkness in the mind doesn't leave.

There are so many spiritual disciplines for the physical form,
Yet the poisons in the mind never give way.

With water, one can wash the body that behaves so badly.
But how will that cleanse the inner wall of imperfection?

O mind
The most exalted and glorious thing you can do
Is to recognize the Divine Reality
In you.

Naanak,
Accepting one's Divinely-Given Identity
Liberates a great many people
Who are lost.

3-4

A person may have so much wisdom,
Yet still be filled with the fear of death.

He may make many different efforts,
But his desires never become satisfied.

Adopting various guises doesn't quench the inner fire.

Millions of remedies,
Yet none succeed in bringing him
To the Divine Court.

There is no way to escape the etheric realms or the shadow worlds.
People become attached to what allures them,
And they burn in Maya's Creative Existence.

All other actions lead
To the punishing experience of Death.

Without appreciating and remembering the Creator,
A person does not receive even a grain of honor.

By calling upon the Divine Reality in every identity,
Suffering goes away.
With ease, Naanak says these things.
And what he speaks pleases the One.

3-5

If you request the four treasures
Of truth, contentment, prosperity, and liberation,

Then bind yourself in service
To those who live with discipline, grace, and purity.

If you long within yourself,
To erase your pain and sorrow,

Then in your heart constantly sing,
Of the Divine Reality that permeates all things.

If you, yourself, seek
Honor and nobility,

Be in the company of those who live a pure life.
Your ego will break.

If you fear birth and death,
Serve those who live
According to the harmony of their own Spirits,
And let them become
Your shelter.

Naanak sacrifices himself
Over and over again

For those people
Who have a thirst to see the Creator.

3-6

Among all people
That person is the greatest leader
Who erases his pride
In the company of those
Who live by purity, grace, and discipline.

Consider that person the highest of all
Who knows within himself
What his weaknesses are.

The mind that becomes the dust
Beneath everyone's feet

Such a mind constantly perceives
The Divine Reality in every heart.

When the darkest, most difficult thoughts
Within the mind get destroyed

Then a person shall look upon the entire Universe
As a beloved friend.

Happiness and sorrow
Become equal in his eyes.

Then, Naanak,
Neither vice nor virtue
Can affect him.

3-7

For those who have nothing,
Experiencing Thy Divine Identity
Makes them wealthy.

For those with no home,
Experiencing Thy Divine Identity
Gives them a place.

For those without honor,
O Cosmic Creative Consciousness,
You become their honor.

O Invisible One,
You bestow your gifts
Upon every being.

Master of the Universe,
You cause every action.

You are the Inner Knower and Guide
In each and every heart.

You alone have the accurate knowledge
Of Your own state and condition.

You dwell in blissful communion
With Your own Creative Self.

Only You
Can appreciate
You.

Naanak,
No one else knows anything.

3-8

Among all spiritual paths,
The most wonderful path
Is to call upon the Divine Reality
In every identity (including your own).

It will purify your deeds.

Among all spiritual actions,
The most exalted action
Is to be in the company of those
Who live by purity, grace, and discipline;

There, a person's false and filthy thoughts
Shall be taken away.

Among all endeavors,
The most excellent endeavor, O my Being,
Is to call upon
The Divine Reality in every identity.

Among all vibrations,
The vibration that reminds you
You are Deathless

Comes from listening
To the Divine's praises
And giving an explanation of them with your tongue.

Among all places,
The highest place of all,

Is that heart, O Naanak,
Where the Divine Identity
Lives.

4

Shalok

O innocent one,
Without virtues or merit,
Always remember the Creator.

Put the One who does everything
In your awareness.

Be with It, Naanak, and become successful.

4

Ashtapadi

4-1

You who live by the Breath of Life,
Contemplate the qualities
Of that Magnificently Beautiful Creator,

Who, from the Beginning,
Made all this visible.

Who fashioned you,
Arranged your existence,
And adorned you.

Who brought you out of the fiery womb.

Who made you drink milk
When you were just a child.

And in the bloom of youth,
Provided food,
A comfortable sense of well-being,
And a sound mind.

When old age happens,
Friends and relatives
Look after you.

The Giver gives you
A place to sit.
Food and drink
For your mouth to enjoy.

O person, devoid of merits,
You don't understand these virtues at all.

Take these things as gifts.
Then, O Naanak,
You shall be successful.

4-2

By Divine Favor,
You live peacefully on the earth,

And you laugh in the company
Of your children, siblings, friends, and spouse.

By Divine Favor,
You drink cool water.

Air and fire—so priceless—
Make you comfortable.

By Divine Favor,
You enjoy all the delights

And every material object
Comes to keep you company.

You have been given hands, feet, ears, eyes, and a tongue.

But you ignore the Creator
And get absorbed in the companionship of others.

In this way,
You become overwhelmed
By your own stupidity
And ignorant mistakes.

O Naanak,
The Creative Master alone
Can pull you out of this.

4-3

From the source of creation
Until the end of time
There is One who Protects and Sustains us.

But the fools don't love that One.

Doing His service, we receive the nine treasures.

Yet, the stupid idiots
Don't apply their minds
To the task.

We are always and forever
In the presence of the Divine Master.

Yet the blind ones consider the Master
To be far, far away.

Doing Divine service, we receive honor
In the Divine Court.

But through foolishness and ignorance,
People forget.

They constantly, constantly make their mistakes.

O Naanak,
The One who Protects and Sustains us
Has no boundaries and no limits.

4-4

Forsaking the jewel,
They seek the company of the bitter.

Abandoning the Ultimate Reality,
They associate with companions
Who lie.

They consider those things permanent
That they will have to leave behind.

What shall happen,
They believe to be many breaths away.

They labor on behalf of what they must walk away from.

And shun the company
Of those who can help.

Washing away the sacred balm
That would deliver them,

They become donkeys who love
To keep company with ashes.

In a well of darkness,
They are fallen, frightened people.

Naanak,
The Creator's compassion can lift them from this state.

4-5

They have the status of a human,
But their actions are like animals.

And they show it to the entire world
Day and night.

Wearing a disguise on the outside
They become dirty on the inside
Focusing on the material world.

Even though they hide things,
Nothing is truly hidden.

Outwardly they display knowledge and meditation,
And they take purifying baths.

Yet inside they are filled
With a dog-like greed.

The fire within
Turns the outer body to ashes.

How can a person swim across this deep ocean,
With such a stone around her neck?

Those people within whom
The Creator lives,

O Naanak,
They effortlessly merge with the Divine.

4-6

How can a person without sight
Deeply listen to find the way?

By holding onto That Hand,
He successfully reaches the end.

Yet how can a person who cannot hear
Understand such a riddle?

Describe the night to him,
He will perceive it as morning.

How can someone without a voice
Sing the most complex spiritual song?

She could put forth a good effort,
But the gods would still disrupt it.

How can a person who cannot walk
Stroll across the mountains?

It's not possible for her to roam those heights.

O Doer of All,
Kind Creator,
I, who have nothing,
Make this request.

Naanak knows,
Only Your Divine Compassion
Delivers a person.

4-7

He doesn't remember
The Divine Helper who keeps him company.

Instead, he loves those
Who fight and oppose him.

He dwells within a house of sand.
And plays at bliss,
Tasting the sweet pleasures
Of the earthly realms.

He accepts firmly in his mind
That this is his true faith.

The fool doesn't pay attention to Death.

Hostility, conflicts,
Sexual desire outside the Divine Will,
Anger,
Attachment;

Lies, distortions,
Incredible greed,
And ill-meaning deceptions;

All of these are his code of conduct,
And in this manner he wiles away
So many lifetimes.

O Naanak,
A person is protected and brought out of this
When the kindness of the Divine
Prevails in his life.

4-8

You, Master of Creation,
We make our prayer to You.

Our bodies, our souls
Everything
Is Your property.

You are our mother and father.
We are Your children.

Through Your kindness,
We receive peace in abundance.

Nobody knows Your limits.

Among the highest,
You are higher still,
Most venerable Divine One.

Your thread holds
Every object in place.

What You arrange and command
Happens.

Only You know
Your true state and condition.

Servant Naanak
Sacrifices himself to You
Forever.

5
Shalok

Having abandoned the Creator,
The Giver of Everything,
He gets attached to other delights.

Naanak says, you can't be successful this way.

Without knowing your Divine Identity,
Honor will leave you.

5

Ashtapadi

5-1

After receiving ten objects,
His confidence gets destroyed
Because of one object he did not receive.

If the one was not given,
And the other ten were taken away, as well,
Then what would this idiot have to say?

No remedy exists
Outside the Master.

Always adore and honor Him.

For the one who attaches her mind
To the Creator's sweetness,
Absolute peace
Rains down on her thoughts.

The person, who, within himself
Trusts and accepts the Divine Plan,

All things come to him, O Naanak.

5-2

You, Yourself, are the Banker
Whose wealth cannot be measured,
And You bestow Your capital upon us.

Eating and drinking,
We use it for our pleasure.

Then, Banker, from the deposit You made,
You take something back,

Causing the ignorant mind
To become angry.

Because of that anger, we lose Your trust
And then our own confidence disappears.

Whatever your capital, place it
Before the One.

Trust and accept
The order of the Creator
On your forehead.

By doing so, you shall flourish
Four times over.

O Naanak,
The Master's kindness
Extends forever.

5-3

Endless are the ways to love Maya,
To love the created reality.

Know with certainty,
All this is temporary.

A person becomes enraptured
With the shade of a tree,

But when that gets destroyed,
Then the mind becomes contrite.

Whatever one sees
Is bound for departure.

We are continuously caught
In a blinding darkness.

The one who fixates
On loving the traveler,

What her hands do
Comes to no purpose.

O mind,
Love the Divine Reality
In every Identity (including your own.)
Peace shall be bestowed upon you.

Naanak,
When the kindness of the Divine prevails,
People focus their attention
On Thee.

5-4

All this is futile
The body, wealth, and family.

Futile the ego,
The sense of ownership
And the enchanting visions
Of the Creative Play.

Futile are kingdoms, youth,
Property and possessions.

Futile and dreadful
Are anger and inappropriate sexual desire.

Futile the chariots, elephants,
Horses and clothing.

Futile the way we watch and enjoy
The Creative Play,
Losing ourselves in its company.

Futile are malice and deceit,
Infatuation and pride.

Futile — placing the self-centered ego above everything,
And acting according to one's fancy.

Stable and effective
Is becoming a lover of the Divine
Under the protection of those who live
By purity, grace, and discipline.

O Naanak,
Repeatedly chanting with devotion and longing
Causes me to live at the Creator's feet.

5-5

Futile the ears that listen to slander about others.

Futile the hand that steals the wealth of others.

Futile the eyes that gaze upon the beauty of another's woman.

Futile the tongue that tastes another's food.

Futile the feet that run to harm others.

Futile the mind that covets, with greed, what another person has.

Futile the body that doesn't help others.

Futile the home that houses distortions.

Without deep understanding,
All that one does is futile.

Fruitful is the body, O Naanak,
That stays focused upon the Divine Reality
Continually present in every Identity.

5-6

Useless—the lifespan of the person
Who focuses on earthly pleasures.

Without understanding the dimension of Ultimate Reality,
How can someone
Experience his own purity?

Useless, the blind body that does not see
Its own Divine Identity.

An unpleasant odor comes out of his mouth.

Without establishing a dialogue
Between one's Infinite Spirit
And the self-in-time-and-space,
The days and nights
Pass uselessly,

As a field dies
Without the rain clouds.

Without singing in appreciation
To the One who sustains the world,
All actions are useless,

Just as wealth
Is pointless to a miser.

Blessed and prosperous forever
Are those people who live in their hearts,
Relating to the Creative Divine Identity
In everything.

For such people, darling one,
Naanak would burn himself
Over and over again.

5-7

People put their energy
Into achieving something besides
A life of spiritual discipline.

There is no love in their minds,
Yet their mouths try to create harmony.

The Master of Creation has the expertise to know
Everything there is to know.

The outer appearance may be that of a yogi,
Yet he is not saturated with Oneness.

A person who instructs others
But does not take action himself

Comes and goes in birth and death.

When he dwells with the Formless One
Within his own being,

Then his spiritual teachings
Help the world swim across.

Those who please You,
O Creator,
They get to know You.

Naanak falls at the feet
Of such a servant.

5-8

To You, O Vast Consciousness,
Who knows all,
I make this humble request.

You, Yourself, do everything
And within Yourself, You enjoy it.

In the dimension of Your own Being,
By Yourself,
You decide and settle all matters.

Some, You cause to think of You
As far away.

Others, You cause to realize
How close You are.

You continue and endure
Independent of all our contrivances
And all of our wisdom.

You know the spiritual discipline of every soul.

Whoever pleases You,
They become attached to Your protective sash.

Within every place,
There is a space,
Where Thou lives, merged.

When You bless someone with Your kindness,
That person becomes Your servant.

Moment to moment,
O Naanak,
Repeat *Hari*,
And continually call upon
The Divine In Action.

6
Shalok

May the fruits of ego:
Anger, greed, attachment
And imbalanced sexual desire
Be destroyed.

The Unseen, Ever-Present Teacher
Blesses Naanak with the gift
Of the Creator's Protection.

6

Ashtapadi

6-1

By Divine favor, you eat so many delicious foods.

Keep the One Master in mind.

By Divine favor, you apply fragrances to your body.

You shall achieve the highest status
When the soul-memory of Infinity
Becomes evident in your personality.

By Divine favor, you dwell peacefully within your home.

Meditate upon this forever in your mind.

By Divine favor, those who dwell in your house
Live with happiness and ease.

Twenty-four hours a day let your speech reflect this.

By Divine favor, you enjoy the taste of Love.

Naanak constantly meditates to achieve union
With what he meditates upon.

6-2

By Divine favor,
You wear fine silk clothes.

Yet somehow, you forsake this truth
And become enticed by something else.

By Divine favor,
You sleep peacefully upon your bed.

O mind, twenty-four hours a day
Sing in a sacred way
About how glorious that is.

By Divine favor,
Everyone respects you.

Let your tongue and your lips
Describe the wonder of it all.

By Divine favor,
You have a spiritual way of life
And a conscious code of conduct.

O mind, always meditate upon
The unique, All-Encompassing Creator.

By lovingly calling upon
The Creator
You shall obtain honor
In the Divine Court.

In this way, Naanak,
You will receive respect
On your journey home.

6-3

By Divine favor, you are healthy.
Your body pure as gold.

Attune yourself with devotion
To the love of the One
Who created the sun and the moon.

By Divine favor, your secrets remain hidden.

O mind, become peaceful
By praising the Divine Reality
Continually present in the Creation.

By Divine favor,
All your flaws and faults get covered.

O mind, the Master of the entire Creation
Is definitely your Protector.

By Divine favor, no one touches you.

Breath after breath, O mind,
Let your inner being and outer being
Vibrate towards the Creator, who is the highest of all.

By Divine favor, you received this rare and precious human form.

O Naanak, become a devotee of it.

6-4

By Divine favor,
You adorn yourself with ornaments.

Mind, why become idle?
Establish the dialogue between your Infinite Spirit
And the self-in-time-and-space.

By Divine favor,
You ride upon horses and elephants.

O mind, never forget
The Creator.

By Divine favor, you have gardens, a domain, and property.

Mind, keep yourself strung on the Creator's thread.

The One who crafted your mind with artistry,

Meditate upon that One always,
Whether sitting or standing.

Meditate upon the Unseen One.

Here and hereafter,
Naanak is under Your Protection.

6-5

By Divine favor, you practice the virtue of being totally giving.

Mind, meditate upon this
Twenty-four hours a day.

By Divine favor,
You conduct your business properly and consciously.

With every breath,
Keep your mind focused upon
The One who Powers the Creation.

By Divine favor,
Your form is radiant, beautiful.

Have an inner dialogue with yourself
About the Creator
Who is always and forever unique.

By Divine favor,
You come from a good family.

Constantly, day and night,
Speak to yourself
About the Creator.

By Divine favor, your honor endures.

Naanak discusses the wonders
That come through the gift of the Teachings.

6-6

By Divine favor,
Your ears deeply listen to *Naad*—
To the creative sound behind the creation

By Divine favor,
Behold the wonder of it all.

By Divine favor,
You speak about the nectar of immortality
With your own tongue.

By Divine favor,
You dwell in the flow of the Universe
With a sense of well-being.

By Divine favor,
Your life becomes perfect, complete
And fruitful.

By Divine favor,
You achieve the most exalted state.

By Divine favor,
You get absorbed into the peaceful flow of the universe.

Yet somehow you abandon the Creator
And become attached to another.

O Naanak,
Through this precious gift of the Guru,
Whose Sound of Wisdom takes you from darkness to light,
The mind wakes up.

6-7

By Divine favor,
You become a light in the world.

Let your mind never forget
The Master of Creation
Who is the root of everything.

By Divine favor,
Your radiance shines.

Hey foolish mind,
Call upon this gift with love.

By Divine favor,
Your duties get completed.

O mind,
Use that knowledge to remain
In the presence of the Divine Light
Always.

By Divine favor,
You enter into the domain of Ultimate Reality.

Oh mind of mine,
Let yourself become absorbed in it.

By Divine favor,
Everyone attains a high status.

O Naanak,
Call upon the Divine with love.
Call upon it out loud
Call upon it within.

6-8

For those who call upon their Divine Identity,
The Divine, Itself, causes the calling.

For those who sing about the virtues of the Divine Reality,
The Divine, Itself, causes the singing.

Through the kindness of the Creator,
Such people become radiant and light.

Through the compassion of the Lord of the Universe,
The lotus of their being
Blossoms.

The mind becomes extraordinarily joyful
When it dwells with the Creator.

And when the Creator's compassion prevails,
Then a person's intelligence becomes the best.

O Master of Everything,
All treasures are within Your Enchanting Creation.

We gain nothing on our own.

A person focuses on the activities
That her Divine Husband has attached her to do.

Naanak,
Nothing is in our hands.

7

Shalok

The Vast, All-Powerful Universal Creator
Is completely beyond what our mind comprehends,
With a depth that cannot be measured.

Whoever speaks about this
Becomes liberated.

Naanak makes this humble request.

Listen deeply, O friend,
To this wondrous description
Of those who lovingly serve the Divine.

7

Ashtapadi

7-1

In the company of those who are spiritually disciplined,
A person's face becomes bright.

Keeping company with those who are spiritually disciplined
Gets rid of all the dirt.

Keeping company with those who are spiritually disciplined,
Ego and pride cease to exist.

Keeping company with those who are spiritually disciplined,
A person's intelligence becomes apparent.

In the company of those who are spiritually disciplined,
One understands that the Creator is near.

Keeping company with those who are spiritually disciplined,
Everything gets settled.

Keeping company with the disciplined and wise,
People obtain the precious jewel of their Divine Identity.

In the company of those who are spiritually disciplined,
One effort matters above all.

What creature of breath
Can fully describe
The greatness of those
Who are disciplined and wise?

O Naanak,
The radiance and beauty of the sages
Comes from their union with the Creator.

7-2

Keeping company with those who are spiritually disciplined,
A person meets the One who is
Beyond the reach of the senses.

In the company of those who are spiritually disciplined,
One's awareness constantly blooms.

In the company of those who are spiritually disciplined,
The five vices become still.

In the company of those who are spiritually disciplined,
One feasts on the sweetness of her Immortal Nature.

In the company of those who are spiritually disciplined,
A person becomes the dust of all.

Keeping company with those who are spiritually disciplined,
One's words become enchanting and beautiful.

Keeping company with those who are spiritually disciplined,
There is nowhere to run.

Keeping company with those who are spiritually disciplined,
The mind becomes consistent and steady.

Keeping company with those who are spiritually disciplined,
A person separates herself from Maya's creative illusion.

In the company of those who are spiritually disciplined,
O Naanak,
The Creator finds happiness.

7-3

In the company of those who are spiritually disciplined,
All enemies become friends.

Being in the company of those who are spiritually disciplined
Is extremely purifying.

In the company of those who are spiritually disciplined,
There is no hostility towards anyone.

Keeping company with those who are spiritually disciplined,
Your feet shall not falter.

In the company of those who are spiritually disciplined,
No one is feeble or slow.

In the company of those who are spiritually disciplined,
A person knows the incredible bliss
That comes from living in-tune with her Divine Identity.

Keeping company with those who are spiritually disciplined,
The afflicting heat of ego dissipates.

Keeping company with those who are spiritually disciplined,
A person surrenders all of himself.

The One within and without knows
The greatness of the sages.

O Naanak, the Creative Master comes to dwell
With those who are disciplined and wise.

7-4

Keeping company with those who are spiritually disciplined,
One never rushes about.

In the company of those who are spiritually disciplined,
A person always finds peace.

In the company of those who are spiritually disciplined,
People experience the Imperceptible One.

In the company of those who are spiritually disciplined,
One tolerates the intolerable.

Keeping company with those who are spiritually disciplined,
A person dwells in the highest state of consciousness.

Keeping company with those who are spiritually disciplined,
A person arrives at the Divine palace.

Keeping company with those who are spiritually disciplined,
People become totally confirmed in Dharma,
In their path of conscious living.

Keeping company with those who are spiritually disciplined,
Realize there is only one Vast, All-Powerful Creator.

Keeping company with those who are spiritually disciplined,
A person receives the treasure of his Divine Identity.

Naanak devotes his service to those
Who live by their spiritual discipline.

7-5

Keeping company with those who are spiritually disciplined,
Liberates all of one's family.

The company of those who are spiritually disciplined
Saves one's companions, friends, and relations.

Keeping company with those who are spiritually disciplined,
A person attains prosperity.

Whoever receives these blessings
Passes those benefits on to everyone.

Even the God of Death serves
The company of the disciplined and wise.

Keeping company with those who are spiritually disciplined,
One can experience the radiance of the transparent, creative energies.

Keeping company with those who are spiritually disciplined,
Clears away the dirt of the subconscious mind.

In the company of those who are spiritually disciplined,
People sing in praise of the nectar
That awakens one's Deathless Nature.

Keeping company with those who are spiritually disciplined
One has access to all places.

O Naanak,
Being in the company of those who are spiritually disciplined
Leads to a fruitful life.

7-6

Keeping company with those who are spiritually disciplined,
There is nothing to work towards.

Seeing this, one receives the gift of happiness.

Keeping company with those who are spiritually disciplined,
Removes one's impurities.

Keeping company with those who are spiritually disciplined,
A person leaves hell behind.

Keeping company with those who are spiritually disciplined,
There is ease here and hereafter.

In the company of those who are spiritually disciplined,
Those who were separate
Get united with the Divine Reality.

One obtains the fruits of one's deepest longing.

Keeping company with those who are spiritually disciplined,
Nothing happens in vain.

That Vast, All-Powerful Creative Consciousness
Lives in the hearts of the sages.

O Naanak,
Listen with complete love
To those who are spiritually disciplined.
It shall liberate you.

7-7

Keeping company with those who are spiritually disciplined,
Deeply listen to your Infinite Identity.

In the company of those who are spiritually disciplined,
Sing, in a sacred way,
About the virtues of the Divine Reality.

Keeping company with those who are spiritually disciplined,
No mind forgets.

In the company of those who are spiritually disciplined,
You will certainly be delivered.

Keeping company with those who are spiritually disciplined,
Attach yourself to the sweetness of the Creator.

In the company of those who are spiritually disciplined,
Behold every single heart.

In the company of those who are spiritually disciplined,
The Divine Order is carried out.

In the company of those who are spiritually disciplined,
There is a state of universal brotherhood and sisterhood.

Keeping company with those who are spiritually disciplined,
All diseases cease to exist.

O Naanak,
It is a priceless gift
To be united with the sages.

7-8

Even the Vedas do not know
The total majesty of those
Who live by discipline, wisdom, and grace.

They can only explain as much as they've heard.

What is praiseworthy in the sages
Is beyond the three qualities.

The entire space of Creation—known and unknown—
Is filled with the praises
Of the disciplined and wise.

The splendor of the sages has no limit.

The splendor of the sages is endless and forever.

The splendor of the sages is the highest of the high.

The splendor of the sages is the greatest of the great.

The splendor of the sages is their success.

O Naanak,
There are no secrets between the spiritually disciplined ones
And the Creator.

8

Shalok

The mind perceives the Ultimate Reality,
The tongue exclaims the Ultimate Reality.

He sees the One
And nothing else.

O Naanak, these are the qualities of a *Braham Giani*—
Of a person with the sensitivity to know Infinity.

8

Ashtapadi

8-1

A person with the sensitivity to know Infinity
Is always neutral,

Like a lotus flower
Untouched by the water it sits upon.

A person with the sensitivity to know Infinity
Is always faultless,

Like the sun that dries everything.

A person with the sensitivity to know Infinity
Beholds all things alike,

Like the life-giving wind,
Which gives its power to both king and beggar.

A person with the sensitivity to know Infinity
Has a singular perseverance,

Like the earth that endures
Those who dig into it,
And those who heal it with sandalwood paste.

A person with the sensitivity to know Infinity
Has this particular quality.
Naanak he is like a fire
That is effortlessly good-natured
To all.

8-2

A person with the sensitivity to know Infinity
Is the purest of the pure,

Like water, to which dirt cannot cling.

There is a light in the mind
Of a person with the sensitivity to know Infinity,

Like the sky over the earth.

To a person with the sensitivity to know Infinity,
Friends and enemies are equal.

A person with the sensitivity to know Infinity
Has no pride or self-conceit.

A person with the sensitivity to know Infinity
Is the highest of the high.

Yet within his own consciousness,
He considers himself
Below all.

Those with the sensitivity to know Infinity
Become servants.

Naanak,
The Creative Master Himself
Is the cause of this.

8-3

A person with the sensitivity to know Infinity
Is the dust under everyone's feet.

A person with the sensitivity to know Infinity
Recognizes the taste of the soul.

A person with the sensitivity to know Infinity
Lives above all illusion.

Nothing bad ever happens because of a person
With the sensitivity to know Infinity.

A person with the sensitivity to know Infinity
Always remains impartial.

The nectar of Immortal Awareness
Rains down wherever
A person with the sensitivity to know Infinity
Directs his gaze.

A person with the sensitivity to know Infinity
Is liberated from her bonds.

A person with the sensitivity to know Infinity
Lives a pure life.

Wisdom is the food of a person
With the sensitivity to know Infinity.

O Naanak,
A person with the sensitivity to know Infinity
Meditates upon the Infinite Creator.

8-4

A person with the sensitivity to know Infinity
Relies on the One above all.

Nothing destroys a person
With the sensitivity to know Infinity.

A person with the sensitivity to know Infinity
Provides for the poor.

A person with the sensitivity to know Infinity
Enthusiastically acts to benefit others.

A person with the sensitivity to know Infinity
Doesn't work for the world.

A person with the sensitivity to know Infinity
Has removed the shackles of a wandering mind.

Whatever happens because of a person
With the sensitivity to know Infinity
Is the absolute best thing that could happen.

A person with the sensitivity to know Infinity
Enjoys the fruits of success.

All those who keep company with a person
Who has the sensitivity to know Infinity
Become liberated.

O Naanak, the entire world
Repeatedly calls upon
A person with the sensitivity to know Infinity.

8-5

A person with the sensitivity to know Infinity
Delights in the One.

A person with the sensitivity to know Infinity
Dwells in the company of the Creator.

A person with the sensitivity to know Infinity
Is nourished by his Divinely-given Identity.

A person with the sensitivity to know Infinity
Considers the Divine Identity within all
As her family.

A person with the sensitivity to know Infinity
Is always awake and aware.

A person with the sensitivity to know Infinity
Abandons the limited ego.

The mind of a person with the sensitivity to know Infinity
Stays in the most exalted state of bliss.

The heart of a person with the sensitivity to know Infinity
Remains continually pleased.

The home of a person with the sensitivity to know Infinity
Embodies an effortless, natural ease.

O Naanak,
Nothing destroys a person
With the sensitivity to know Infinity.

8-6

A person with the sensitivity to know Infinity
Truly knows the Creator.

A person with the sensitivity to know Infinity
Loves to keep company with the One.

A person with the sensitivity to know Infinity
Becomes carefree.

A person with the sensitivity to know Infinity
Has a clear, pure intellect.

The Creator, Itself, causes a person
To become sensitive enough to know Infinity.

A person with the sensitivity to know Infinity
Has an amazing brilliance.

By tremendous good fortune,
One gets to look into the eyes
Of a person with the sensitivity to know Infinity.

I offer myself as a sacrifice,
Time and again,
To the person with the sensitivity to know Infinity.

The Divine Being known as Shiva
Searches for a person with the sensitivity
To know Infinity.

Naanak,
A person with the sensitivity to know Infinity
Is himself the Supreme Divine Lord.

8-7

It is impossible to determine the worth
Of a person with the sensitivity to know Infinity.

Everything is understood by a person
With the sensitivity to know Infinity.

Who knows the secrets of a person
With the sensitivity to know Infinity?

I constantly salute
The one who has the sensitivity to know Infinity.

There is no way to describe
A person with the sensitivity to know Infinity
By even half a syllable.

A person with the sensitivity to know Infinity
Is Master of all.

Who can explain the pure wisdom that comes from
A person with the sensitivity to know Infinity?

Only a person with the sensitivity to know Infinity
Understands the condition of someone like himself.

There are no boundaries, no end
For a person with the sensitivity to know Infinity.

Naanak always bows with honor
To the one who has the sensitivity to know Infinity.

8-8

A person with the sensitivity to know Infinity
Is the Creator of the whole world.

A person with the sensitivity to know Infinity
Lives forever and never dies.

A person with the sensitivity to know Infinity
Is the one who gives life, the path in life,
And liberation.

A person with the sensitivity to know Infinity
Is the complete and perfect Primal Being
Who bestows the rewards.

A person with the sensitivity to know Infinity
Is the Master of those who have no master.

A person with the sensitivity to know Infinity
Extends a protective hand over everyone.

A person with the sensitivity to know Infinity
Can cast his consciousness into any form.

A person with the sensitivity to know Infinity
Is herself beyond form.

Only a person with the sensitivity to know Infinity
Can create another person with the same radiance and beauty.

O Naanak, a person with the sensitivity to know Infinity
Gives prosperity to all.

9

Shalok

Those who, within themselves,
Focus their hearts
On their Divine Identity

See the Respected One
In all.

Moment to moment,
They perceive the Great Master,
And greet Him with love and affection.

O Naanak,
People with this consciousness
Live unaffected
And they save everyone.

9

Ashtapadi

9-1

His tongue will not touch a false statement.

Beholding the world as it is
With a pure vision
Love comes into his mind.

His eyes do not look upon a woman's physical form.

In the company of those who live purely,
He deeply loves to serve the wise.

Her ears do not listen to negativity and slander.

Among everyone, she knows herself to be
The weakest of all.

By the grace of the Sound of Wisdom,
She turns away from poison.

She removes the thoughts
From the container of her mind.

By conquering the senses,
He restrains the five flaws
(Of pride, anger, attachment, lust, and greed.)

O Naanak,
Among so many millions,
Those who have these attributes
Are considered pure and unaffected.

9-2

Consider a person a devotee of Vishnu
If he can rise above and be happy.

He separates himself
From Vishnu's creative play.

He performs his duty
Without any thought of reward.

Such a devotee of Vishnu
Walks a path of pure Dharma.

He does not long for the fruits of his desires.

The Lover of the One gets absorbed
In the company of sacred music.

Within his body and mind,
He meditatively communicates
With the Preserver of the World.

He is kind and benevolent to everyone.

With a firmness of mind,
He repeatedly calls upon his Divine Identity
And inspires other to do so.

O Naanak, such a devotee of Vishnu
Obtains the highest status.

9-3

The Beloved of the Divine One
Is dyed in devotion.

She abandons, completely,
The company of the wicked.

She destroys all doubts from within her own mind.

And she worships the totality
Of the Vast, All-Powerful Creator.

In the company of those who live
By purity, grace, and discipline,
The dirt of her incorrect actions departs.

Such a Beloved has the best understanding,
And she constantly, constantly serves the Divine.

With affection,
She bestows her body and mind
Upon the Lord who preserves her.

The feet of the Divine
Live in her heart.

O Naanak, in this way
A person receives the status
Of becoming the Divine One's Beloved.

9-4

The learned spiritual person
Is one who chastises his own mind,

Who deeply searches,
Within his soul,
For the Divine Identity that created
The sun and the moon.

And from the Divine Identity
That created the sun and the moon,
He drinks the nectar of understanding.

The instructions of such a learned spiritual person
Liberate the world.

The stories of the Divine
Dwell in his heart.

Such a learned spiritual person
Does not return to the womb again.

He completely comprehends
The root of all sacred scriptures.

In the subtle experiences,
He knows what is solid.

He instructs all levels of society.

Naanak forever honors and bows
To such a learned spiritual person.

9-5

In the Seed Mantra—
Sa-Ta-Na-Ma—
All knowledge exists.

Those who lovingly repeat it,
No matter what their station in life,
Will experience their Divine Identity.

Whoever repeats it with devotion
Will realize the state of freedom.

Some people attain this
In the company of those who live by purity, grace, and discipline.

Through the kindness of the Divine,
They focus on it in their hearts.

This mantra will carry across
Animals, ghosts, and those stupid as stone.

The Divine Identity cures all diseases.

Joyfully singing about the virtues of the Divine,
One becomes the very form of happiness.

A person cannot experience Dharma
Just by any method.

Naanak, those for whom it has been written
Since the beginning of time
Are the ones who intermix themselves with it.

9-6

When the Vast, All-Powerful Creator
Makes Its home in a person's mind,

Then such a person identifies himself
As a true servant of the Divine.

He beholds the very being of the Creator
As his own Soul.

This servant loves to deliver the service.

He knows the Divine Presence
Is forever and constantly near.

Such a servant is accepted into the Divine Court.

When the Divine, Itself, extends Its kindness to the person who serves,

Then the servant finds the Totality
Within his own awareness and understanding.

Such a soul remains detached,
Even in the company of others.

In this way, Naanak becomes Ram Das,
Servant to the One who created the sun and the moon.

9-7

The soul that loves the command
Of the Creator

Is definitely considered
Liberated while alive.

He feels cheerful,
Then he feels grief.

Yet, he never experiences separation,
And remains in the bliss of his soul's reflection.

He has gold,
Then he has clay.

He has nectar,
Then he gets poison.

He is honored,
Then dishonored.

He is poor,
Then a king.

Whoever applies himself to such a way of life,

O Naanak,
That Divine Man
Is called Liberated-While-Alive.

9-8

All places belong
To the One who Oversees the Entire Creation.

In those homes that keep this spirit,
The Divine Identity exists.

In a state of union,
The Divine, Itself, does everything
And causes everything to be done.

Only those events take place,
Which please the Creator.

Divine One, You expand Yourself
Into limitless pulses of energy.

The colors of the One who Transcends and Creates
Cannot be fully grasped.

When someone is given the intellect to understand this,
Then that person blooms.

The Vast, All-Powerful Creator
Is the Indestructible Doer,

And is endlessly, endlessly, endlessly kind.

O Naanak,
Establish a continuous dialogue
Between your Infinite Spirit and the self-in-time-and-space.
This will bring you happiness.

10

Shalok

Countless servants praise the Divine—
Their numbers are endless, without limit.

O Naanak,
This creation the Master created
Has many ways and numerous methods.

10

Ashtapadi

10-1

Millions worship and adore You.
Millions engage in the business of good behavior.
Millions dwell by sacred waters.
Millions live in doubt as renunciates in the forest.
Millions listen to sacred texts.
Millions purify themselves through the inner fire.
Millions meditate with one-pointed concentration on the soul.
Millions understand You through spiritual poetry.
Millions meditate on Your New Names.
Naanak, the Divine Doer's domain
Is endless.

10-2

Millions live in pride.
Millions are blind and ignorant.
Millions of misers act cruelly.
Millions are young souls without impact.
Millions steal the wealth of others.
Millions create pain for those around them.
Millions labor on behalf of the temporal plane.
Millions wander in foreign lands.

People are attached
To whatever You
Engage them to do.

Naanak,
The Creator knows the purpose
For the creation It has fashioned.

10-3

Millions are celibates, yogis, and spiritually wise.
Millions are kings, sensualists, and enjoyers of pleasure.
So many millions of birds and snakes have been created.
So many millions of stones and trees have been produced.
There are so many millions of winds, waters, and fires.
So many millions of lands, elements, and orbs in the sky.
There are so many millions of suns, moons, and stars.

So many millions of gods, demons
And Kings of Heaven with canopies above their heads.

Everything has been securely placed on the thread of the Divine.

O Naanak,
Those who please the One, they are the people who are saved.

10-4

Millions of creatures
Are comprised of the three qualities:
Raajas: fiery and active
Taamas: heavy and slow
Saatvak: subtle and pure.

Millions of sacred writings and mystical texts exist.

There are ten million jewels of learning
In ten million oceans of existences.

There are millions of beings
With very different manners.

Millions live a really long life.
Millions of mountains become gold.

There are millions of demi-gods, ghosts,
And divine angels singing in the court of heaven.

Millions of dead bodies, haunting spirits,
Teachers of demons, and eaters of flesh exist.

All are close,
Yet all of them are so far away.

O Naanak,
The Divine One, Itself,
Is overflowing
Yet untouched.

10-5

Millions live in the underworld.
Millions reside in heaven and in hell.
Millions take birth, live their lives, then die.
Millions cycle back into the womb many more times.
Millions just sit there and eat.
Millions labor to the point of exhaustion.
Millions are wealthy and blessed.
Millions dwell anxiously in the temporal plane.
Everyone is placed where it pleases Thee, Divine One.
O Naanak, all things are in the hands of the Creator.

10-6

Millions turn their back on the world
And devote themselves to the Divine.

With adoration, they cling to the companionship
Of the Cosmic Identity who created the sun and the moon.

Millions seek out the Divine Master.

Within one's soul, the Vast, All-Powerful Creator is discovered.

Millions thirst for a sight of the Divine Lord.

They join themselves to Him, the Indestructible Creative One.

Millions beg to be part of the community who practices truth.

They dye themselves in the color of the Vast, All-Powerful Creator.

Those for whom this happens
Feel totally delighted.

Naanak, such servants are forever blessed and prosperous.

10-7

Millions of beings eat
In millions of realms.

Millions of Creators exist
In millions of heavens.

There are millions of Divine Personalities.

So many involved in the show.

Many, many times the Creation has spread far in its expansion.

Forever and forever, there is just One—*Ek Ong Kaar.*
One Spirit Beyond moving within the Creation,
Coordinating, consolidating, continually creating.

Millions have acted in so many different ways.

The Divine Master causes this,
And back into the Divine Master they merge.

No one can know His limits.

O Naanak,
The Creative Consciousness absolutely lives
As ItSelf within ItSelf.

10-8

There are millions who serve
The Vast, All-Powerful Creator.

By doing this, their souls radiate light.

There are millions who know
The essence of reality.

They constantly perceive the One with their own eyes.

Millions drink the nectar of their Divine Identity.

They attain immortality
And indeed live always and forever.

Millions sing about
The virtues of the Divine Identity.

They merge into the taste of their own soul
And flow with life, in peace.

Those who are servants of the One Creative Consciousness
Remember It with every breath.

O Naanak,
They are the Beloved of the Divine Lord.

11

Shalok

There is One Creator
Who causes all actions.
A second force does not exist.

O Naanak, let me devote myself to that Divine Power
Who supports the water, the land, and the expanse of the world.

11

Ashtapadi

11-1

The Omnipotent Divine One
Causes all the deeds to be done.

Only what pleases the Divine happens.

In a moment, something gets established,
Then destroyed.

No boundaries exist to define Thy end.

By Divine Command, the entire creation gets supported.
Yet, the Divine exists beyond any support.

By Divine Command, there is birth.
By Divine Command, there is union.

By Divine Command, there is exalted work,
And work that is lowly.

By Divine Command, there are so many colors.

The Divine Itself creates,
Then beholds the greatness of Its own creation.

Naanak, the One has merged Itself with everything.

11-2

By the Creator's pleasure,
One acquires the status of a human being.

By the Creator's pleasure,
A stone is made to swim across.

By the Creator's pleasure,
A person's life will be protected, even without breath.

When it pleases the Creator,
Someone speaks about the Divine Reality.

By the Creator's pleasure,
Those who have fallen away from the path become liberated.

The One Itself does,
And within Itself understands the reasons why.

The Divine Itself created duality
And has mastery over both sides.

The One who knows the secrets of every heart
Plays with joy.

Whatever pleases Thee
Those deeds get accomplished.

O Naanak,
There is no one else to see.

11-3

How can what a person says ever happen?

Only what pleases the Divine gets accomplished.

Everything would be taken, if left in people's hands.

Whatever pleases the Divine
Is the only thing that occurs.

People become absorbed in ignorance and vice.

If they learn about the Cosmic Consciousness,
Then that Cosmic Consciousness will save them.

They run around in the ten directions,
Deluded and in doubt.

Their minds wander in circles every moment.

When the One acts with kindness,
It gives a person the gift of devotional love.

O Naanak,
Then such a servant gets blended
With her Divine Identity.

11-4

In a moment, the lowly insect becomes a king.

The Vast, All-Powerful Creator cherishes the poor and the humble.

Those who are not perceived by anyone—
The invisible—

Become clearly seen, instantly,
Across the ten directions.

The Divine bestows Its blessings upon them.

The Master of the World
Does not consider their accounts.

All the bodies and souls
Are the investment capital of the One.

In every heart, the Great Creative Consciousness
Shines perfectly.

You, Yourself, have crafted Your own forms.
Naanak lives to behold Thy wonders.

11-5

No power exists in anyone's hands.

The Divine One causes the deeds to be done,
And pulls everyone along by a string through the nose.

These dear souls are helpless—
They act out the command.

People only become what pleases Thee.

Sometimes, a person lives in an elevated way.
Sometimes, in a very lowly state.

Sometimes grieving.
Sometimes laughing, dyed with delight.

Sometimes, a person has negative, slanderous thoughts.

Sometimes, they go up to the heavens,
Then descend to the underworld.

Sometimes, a person comes to know and understand
The Vast, All-Powerful Creator.

O Naanak,
The Divine Itself
Causes us to meet It.

11-6

Sometimes, people perform many different styles of dance.
Sometimes, they remain extremely still day and night.
Sometimes, they exhibit a mighty, terrifying anger.
Sometimes, they become the dust of all.
Sometimes, a person presides as a noble king.
Sometimes, he is fashioned as a lowly beggar.
Sometimes, a person calls slander upon himself.
Sometimes, people speak about him in the most excellent ways.

A person stays where the Creator puts her.

Through the blessing that comes from the Sound of Wisdom,
Naanak speaks this truth.

11-7

Sometimes, people become learned and spiritual
Talking about what they know.
Sometimes, people silently focus on meditation.
Sometimes, they take their baths along the bank of a river.
Sometimes, the saints and sages have faces filled with wisdom.
Sometimes, the Divine takes on the life of an insect,
An elephant, or a worm.
In various births, he lives in doubt and delusion.
Observe the soul acting in these humble forms.
The dances take place this way, according to the Creator's pleasure.

Whatever the One likes,
Is the only thing that happens.

O Naanak,
There is no one else.

11-8

Sometimes, people come to live in the company of the sages.

They do not leave that place.

Wisdom blossoms from within themselves.

That place does not get destroyed.

Their bodies and minds become dyed with the singular color
Of their Divine Identity.

And they forever dwell in the company
Of the Vast, All-Powerful Creator.

Just as water gets absorbed into water,

So the Light of the being merges into the Light of the community.

The tendency to wander gets erased and destroyed.
A person attains the state of repose.

Naanak forever offers himself as a sacrifice to the Creator.

12

Shalok

The humble and poor who restrain themselves dwell in peace.
But the great and the mighty egocentric people, Naanak,
Melt in their pride.

12

Ashtapadi

12-1

Those who, within themselves,
Have the pride of a king
Fall into hell and live the life of a dog.

The ones who know, "I am beautiful and young,"
Become creatures reborn in excrement.

Whoever talks about the good deeds they have done,
Will wander lost in the womb through many births and deaths.

Those who take pride in their wealth and their land,
Are foolishly blind and ignorant.

When Your kindness prevails,
The heart becomes humble.

Such a heart, O Naanak, is liberated and finds peace hereafter.

12-2

People become egomaniacs when wealth comes to them.
Yet nothing equal to a blade of grass
Will accompany them when they go.

Whoever places his hopes
On scores of armies and servants
Is destroyed in an instant.

The one who believes he has power over everything
Is reduced to ashes in a moment.

Those who pridefully refuse to approve of anyone else,
Will get humiliated and disgraced by the ruling hand of Dharma.

Naanak, by the sweet gift of the Teachings,
Pride is erased.

Those servants, O Naanak, are embraced in the Court of Divinity.

12-3

When a person performs millions of ritual actions
And claims, "I did it"—
All that labor is in vain.

When someone pridefully does many acts of self-purification,
She will continue to incarnate in heaven and in hell.

A person may make so many efforts,
Yet the sense of self does not soften.

How can such a one sing and talk about
The Court of the Divine Presence?

Nothing noble will come near the one
Who speaks highly of himself.

Says Naanak, the mind that becomes the dust of all
Is absolutely pure.

12-4

When someone believes that what he knows
Causes something to happen,
Then happiness will never come to him.

When through his knowledge, he claims, "I did it,"
Then he is reborn because of his pride.

When someone sees another as an enemy or a friend,
Then his mental understanding lacks steadiness.

When someone, through attachment,
Gets involved with the company of Illusion,

Then the ruling hand of Dharma
Shall bestow the consequences.

Through the kindness of the Creator,
The bonds break.

By the sweet gift of the Teachings,
People get released from their egos.

12-5

After earning thousands, he wakes up and chases hundreds of thousands.
But satisfaction doesn't come to him.
He only attains Illusion.

There is no satisfaction at all.
He is consumed and consumed until he dies.

Indulging in so many sensual pleasures poisons him.

Without contentment, no one can rule.

All his work is useless and vain—
Like desires in a dream.

Total happiness and peace come from loving one's Divine Identity.

This happens to someone by great good-fortune.

You, within Yourself, Divine One,
Do everything that is done.

Naanak always and forever repeats, *Har,*
Calling upon the Divine Reality.

12-6

The One who is the Doer
Causes all the deeds to be done.

How can the hand of a person do anything?

Things unfold according to how the Divine One perceives it.

The Creator
Is absolutely by Itself
And continually within Itself.

Whatever the Master loves,
That is the thing He does.

He is far away from everyone,
And with everyone keeps company.

The Divine deeply understands,
Observes,
And has insight into what is truly happening.

Thou, within Thyself, are One.
Thou, within Thyself, are many.

You are not destroyed by death.
You do not come and go.

O Naanak,
The Divine permeates through everything
Indeed forever.

12-7

The Divine, Itself, provides the instructions.
The Divine, Itself, becomes realized.

The Divine, Itself, creates
And stays with the entire Creation.

This expansive show belongs to the One who has fashioned it.

Every single thing belongs to the Great Doer.
What exists that can be considered separate?

The One is absolutely
In the inner-space of any place.

The Creative Doer, within Itself,
Is the cause of all Its marvels.

It is the Force behind this wondrous show,
Limitless in Its delightful expression.

Within the mind, the Divine exists.
And within the Divine Consciousness, the mind exists.

O Naanak,
There is no end to what can be said
About Thy worth.

12-8

True, true, and ever true
Is the Master Creator.

Through the sweet gift of the Teachings,
A person can explain this.

All that is done is real,
Absolutely real.

Among millions of people,
Some rare person recognizes this.

Noble, noble, and ever noble
Is Thy form, Divine One.

Extremely beautiful You are—
Boundless and unique.

Pure, pure, and ever pure
Is the frequency of Thy Divine Words

The ears hear these Words in the beat of the heart,
And understand their meaning.

Sacred, sacred, and ever sacred
Is the life of purity.

With love in the mind,
Naanak repeats the *Naam*—
Calling upon his Divine Identity.

13
Shalok

The one who seizes the protection of the saints
Becomes liberated.

Those who slander the saints, O Naanak, are reborn again and again.

13

Ashtapadi

13-1

Causing trouble to a saint[4]
Reduces the span of one's life.

A person can't escape rebirth
When he causes trouble to a saint.

Causing trouble to a saint,
All comforts leave.

Causing trouble to a saint,
A person lives in hell.

Causing trouble to a saint,
One's thoughts become dirty.

Causing trouble to a saint,
Honorable people become low.

No one can protect the one who kills a saint.

Wherever trouble is created for a saint,
That place becomes soiled.

If a saint acts from benevolence and grace,
Then, O Naanak.

The slanderer is made to swim across,
By being in the saint's company.

---

[4]   Saint. In the 14th Ashtapadi, 5th verse, Guru Arjan provides a definition of a saint as a person within whose awareness the Creator has entered. "When the Divine Reality and the Creator/Enter into someone's mental awareness,/Then that person becomes an easy-going saint/Who never wavers."

13-2

Causing trouble to a saint
One's face becomes twisted.

Causing trouble to a saint,
A person becomes a cackling crow.

Causing trouble to a saint,
One is reborn as a snake.

Causing trouble to a saint,
One takes rebirth as a crawling worm.

Causing trouble to a saint,
A person burns in her desires.

The one who causes trouble to a saint
Deceives everybody.

Causing trouble to a saint
A person loses the total radiance of her being.

Causing trouble to a saint,
One becomes the lowest of the low.

The one who harms a saint
Doesn't belong anywhere.

O Naanak, if it pleases the saint,
Such people shall be saved.

13-3

The one who speaks negatively about a saint
Is a mighty tyrant.

The one who speaks negatively about a saint
Does not receive a moment's rest.

The one who speaks negatively about a saint
Is a great killer.

The Supremely Divine Destroyer punishes the one
Who slanders the saints.

The one who speaks negatively about a saint
Has no kingdom.

The one who speaks negatively about a saint
Lives in pain and poverty.

The one who speaks negatively about a saint
Contracts all diseases.

The one who speaks negatively about a saint
Remains separate from the Divine forever.

The one who speaks negatively about a saint
Has committed the gravest mistake of all.

O Naanak,
If it pleases the saint
Then such people become liberated.

13-4

The one who finds fault with a saint
Is forever impure.

The one who finds fault with a saint
Is no one's friend.

There is a punishment given
To the one who finds fault with a saint.

Everyone abandons the person
Who finds fault with a saint.

The one who finds fault with a saint
Is extremely proud.

The one who finds fault with a saint
Always acts immoral.

The one who finds fault with a saint
Lives and dies.

Peace ignores the one
Who causes trouble to a saint.

The one who finds fault with a saint
Has no place.

O Naanak,
If it pleases the saint,
He will meet with such a person.

13-5

The one who finds fault with a saint
Is broken in half from within.

The work of one who finds fault with a saint
Shall never get completed.

The one who finds fault with a saint
Wanders in a jungle of delusion.

The one who finds fault with a saint
Is empty inside.

He is a being without breath,
A dead corpse.

The one who finds fault with a saint
Has no roots anywhere.

Whatever that person sows
Is what she shall eat.

No one will become the Protector of a person
Who finds fault with a saint.

O Naanak, if it pleases the saint,
Such people shall be saved.

13-6

The one who finds fault with a saint
Cries in the end,

Like a fish without water,
Writhing in pain.

The one who finds fault with a saint
Starves, bereft of his kingdom,

Just as fire is not satisfied
By the firewood it is given.

The one who finds fault with a saint
Is left abandoned and alone,

Like a barren sesame plant
Grieving for its seeds in the field.

The one who finds fault with a saint
Is kept from Dharma, the path of spiritual law.

The one who finds fault with a saint
Always speaks falsely

From the beginning of time,
The work of the slanderer was ordained.

O Naanak,
People only become
What pleases the Divine.

13-7

The one who finds fault with a saint,
His body becomes deformed.

The one who finds fault with a saint
Deals with the consequences of her actions
In the court of the Divine.

The one who finds fault with a saint
Lives in a state of endless longing.

The one who finds fault with a saint
Neither dies nor has a purpose for living.

The hopes of those who find fault with a saint
Are not fulfilled.

The one who finds fault with a saint
Leaves this life joylessly.

The one who finds fault with a saint
Cannot rest.

He acts according to his own pleasure,
And that is what he becomes.

Nothing can erase the consequences of his actions.

Naanak,
Only the True One
Understands this.

13-8

All the hearts belong
To the One who is the Doer.

Adore that Doer
Forever and ever.

Day and night,
Speak the praises
Of the Creator.

Meditate upon that Power
With every breath and with every bite of food.

The Divine puts everything to use
That It makes.

Everything becomes what it is created to become.

The play is Yours,
And You are the Doer.

Who else can understand it,
Or speak about it?

By Your kindness,
You give someone the experience
Of her Divine Identity.

Such people, O Naanak,
Are incredibly blessed.

14

Shalok

Abandon your cleverness and intellect, Divine ones.

When you practice *Simran*—
The art of establishing a dialogue
Between the Infinite Spirit and the self-in-time-and-space—
Then you will know the presence of the Royal Divine Reality.

I only have one wish.

To keep that Divine Reality in mind.

Then, Naanak,
Suffering, doubt, and fear will depart.

14

Ashtapadi

14-1

It is pointless for a human being to rely
Upon all the knowledge that exists.

There is only One Honorable Creator who is the Giver.

Whoever receives His gifts
Becomes completely satisfied.

No desires cling to that person.

The One Itself destroys,
And the One Itself protects.

Nothing is in a person's hands.

Peace happens when we deeply understand
That life moves according to the Divine Plan.

Thread the Divine Identity around your throat.

Establish a dialogue between your Infinite Spirit
And the self-in-time-and-space,
And keep the dialogue going to realize the Creator.

Then, Oh Naanak,
No obstacle can touch you.

14-2

Within your mind, appreciate the Formless One.

O mind of mine,
Make truth your business.

Drink in the pure taste of the nectar
That awakens you
To your own Immortality.

Then, dear soul,
You will receive eternal happiness.

Your eyes will behold the color of the Divine Master.

Be in the company of those who live by wisdom and grace.
Let all other relationships go.

My feet walk the path of *Gobind*—the Protector.

By repeating *Har* for even a little while
And calling upon the Divine Reality,
The blocks in the subconscious mind get released.

Engage in the work the Divine Reality has called you to do,
And listen to Its stories.

Then, O Naanak, your forehead will become radiant and light,
In the Divine Court.

14-3

The servants of the Divine who have come into the world
Are extremely fortunate.

They sacredly sing, always and forever,
About the virtuous qualities of the Divine Reality.

They discuss, to the point of understanding,
The Identity of the One who created the sun and the moon.

In this world,
Such people are considered truly blessed and prosperous.

With their minds, bodies, and mouths,
They communicate from the heart about the Divine Reality.

The know happiness and peace,
Forever and always.

They recognize the One,
Just the One,
Only One.

The awareness of this knowledge serves them
In this world and the next.

Those minds that keep company with the Divine Identity
Practice acceptance and obedience.

Naanak, such people understand purity.

14-4

Through the gift of the Teachings,
A person understands the Self within the self.

Through this knowing,
Her desires get extinguished.

In the company of those who live by purity, grace, and discipline,
Such a person discusses the majesty
Of the unending Divine Reality.

For those who serve this Divine Reality,
All diseases come to an end.

Day and night, such a one
Only explains the sacred songs
That offer spiritual guidance.

Living a householder's life,
She honestly achieves
The final state of emancipation.

The servant who places her highest hopes
On the One Supreme Consciousness

Cuts off the noose
From the messenger of death.

She whose mind hungers
For the Vast, All-Powerful Creator

Is not tied to misery, O Naanak.

14-5

When the Divine Reality and the Creator
Enter into someone's mental awareness,

Then that person becomes an easy-going saint
Who never wavers.

When the Creator, Himself,
Bestows His kindness,

Then how, pray tell, could His devoted servant
Have anything to fear?

This is the manner in which a person with subtle understanding sees life.

The Divine, Itself, is merged in Its own work.

Correcting and purifying Itself,
Correcting and purifying,
Correcting and purifying,
It becomes successful.

Through the sweet gift of the Teachings,
Someone totally understands this fundamental truth.

Seeing this,
It becomes the root of everything.

O Naanak,
Then the subtle, refined knowing
Becomes completely real.

14-6

Nothing is born and nothing dies.

You, Yourself, marvel at what You alone have created.

Coming and going is just moving between
The seen and the unseen.

The whole world flows according to the Divine Command.

The Divine One, within Itself,
Is also the Self within everything.

There are various paths that the Creator has fashioned—
Establishing them and then dissolving them.

Yet the One remains Indestructible
In the realm where nothing exists at all.

The One is the support
That sustains the Universe.

It is Unobserved,
Undifferentiated,
The Perfect Protector
And radiant.

Naanak repeatedly calls upon the Divine,
Because the Divine has caused him to do so.

14-7

The one who knows the Creator
Becomes noble and honorable.

By his counsel,
The whole world is freed.

The servant of the Creator
Liberates everyone.

The servant of the Creator
Helps others forget their trouble and pain.

The Divine, in Its benevolence,
Has merged Itself with them.

They flourish with happiness
By meditating on the Sound Current that cuts the ego,
Given by the Teacher of Wisdom.

Those that selflessly serve
And cling to that service,

Are extraordinarily fortunate.
The Divine has touched them with kindness.

By repeatedly calling upon one's Divine Identity,
A person receives comfort and ease.

O Naanak,
Give such people the highest respect.

14-8

Whatever the devotees do,
They do it because they love the Creator.

Always and forever,
They dwell in the company of the Divine Reality.

Whatever happens for them, happens with ease,
According to the pleasure of the Divine.

They absolutely recognize the One
Who causes all actions.

Whatever the Creator does,
They find the sweetness in it.

They see the subtlety of the Divine
In everything that exists.

They originate from the One into whom they merge.

They are the treasures of peace,
For that is what they were made to be.

By honoring Its devotees,
The Divine One honors Itself.

O Naanak,
Know that the Creator and His servants are one.

15

Shalok

The All-Powerful Creator
Is completely present,
And knows everyone's pain and misery.

By establishing a dialogue with the Master,
People become liberated.

Naanak offers himself as a sacrifice to the One.

15

Ashtapadi

15-1

The Sustainer of the World
Mends what is broken.

It nurtures and protects all the beings.

Within Its mind, the Divine has concern for everyone.

Through the Divine, no one becomes distressed.

O my mind, always repeat *Har*
And call upon the Divine Reality within all things.

The Creator is completely indestructible
And abides within Its own Self.

Nothing happens except
What the Divine One does.

O being of breath, even if you long for hundreds of things,

Without the One, none of your work gets done.

Naanak, redemption comes by reciting and calling upon
The One Divine Identity that seeds the Creation.

15-2

Do not use your lovely appearance
To captivate and enchant people.

The Creator's light
Shines beautifully in every heart.

Why be proud of your wealth?

All of your property and prosperity
Has come to you as a gift.

Someone may be called
Boundlessly brave.

But without the skillful artistry of the Creator,
How can that person even move?

If someone were to preside as the Great Giver,

Know such a "Giver" is simply a fool.

Through the blessing of the Sound of Wisdom,
A person breaks through the sickness of ego.

O Naanak, such people are healthy forever.

15-3

As a pillar gives support to the home,

So the Sound Current that guides the spirit and cuts the ego
Shores up the mind.

As a stone, by boarding a boat,
Is made to cross the water,

So the one who lives by breath
Is saved by attaching herself
To the Teacher's feet.

As a lantern illuminates the darkness,
So catching a sight of the Teacher
Brings ecstasy to the mind.

One may come across a path through a great forest.

Similarly, joining the company of those who are disciplined and wise
Allows the Divine Light to make Itself known.

They who seek the dust of the spiritual people,

Their longing for the Divine Reality is fulfilled, O Naanak.

15-4

O foolish mind, why do you weep?

You receive what has been written in your destiny,
According to your past actions.

The Creator is the Giver of difficulties and of peace.

Abandon everything else.
Think and care about the One.

Whatever the Creator does,
Trust it and be at peace.

Why become deluded and wander in ignorance?

What came with you into this life?

You are a greedy worm who has become coiled around
The taste of your own desires.

Within your heart, call upon
The Identity of the One who made the sun and the moon.

O Naanak, then you shall return home with honor.

15-5

The commodity which you have come to acquire,
Is the Identity of the One who created the sun and the moon.
You will find it in the home of spiritual people.

Abandon your pride.
Take the value of your mind,

And within your heart, weigh the Identity of the One
Who made the sun and the moon.

Load up this merchandise,
And walk in the company of those who live by love and grace.

Forsake all that entangles you in poison.

Then everyone will bless you.

Your face will become absolutely radiant
In the court of the Divine.

This business is done by some rare one.

Naanak dedicates himself in service
To such a person forever.

15-6

Wash the feet of those who meditate,
And drink the washing water.

Devote your very life to those who live by love and grace.

Take the dust of the sages,
And purify yourself with it.

Sacrifice yourself to those
Who are disciplined and wise.

Service to the sages comes by tremendous good fortune.

In the company of the wise people,
Sing songs about the Divine.

Those who live by discipline and grace
Shall protect you from so many blocks.

Sing about the virtues of the Divine,
And enjoy the taste of your own Immortal Nature.

Enter the portal of those who live in the purity of their own spirits,
And take shelter there.

Naanak, in that place,
You shall receive
Every peace and comfort.

15-7

The All-Powerful Creator
Bestows life upon the dead.

The Divine Subtle Being
Gives nourishment to the hungry.

All the treasures
Abide in the Light of the Divine's eyes.

According to your past actions,
You gain what has been written for you.

Everything is done by the One
In a state of union.

Without the One,
Nothing and no one else
Can cause anything to happen.

O student,
Day and night,
Forever and always,
Repeat this to yourself.

This is the absolute highest and purest action of all.

By Your kindness, Creator,
You give someone the experience of her Divine Identity.

In this manner, O Naanak,
A person becomes pure.

15-8

The one whose mind completely trusts the Sound of Wisdom,

Comes to understand the Creator
And It's Creative Essence.

All those who love the Divine
Are heard about in the three worlds.

The person within whose heart
The One abides,

Her actions are authentic
And her way of life is true.

When the experience of the Ultimate Reality
Lives in a person's heart,
Then he speaks truth with his mouth.

He directly perceives the Ultimate Reality,
Beholding the Ultimate Truth within the form of Creation.

True is the expanse of existence.
True is its purpose.

When the Vast, All-Powerful Creator
Reveals the Ultimate Reality to someone,

Naanak, such a person merges with Truth.

16

Shalok

The Creator is separate from the three qualities.
It has neither form nor outline nor color.

Through the One, a person becomes realized,
This happens, O Naanak, through Divine delight.

16

Ashtapadi

16-1

Keep the Indestructible Creator in your thoughts.

Forsake your love of the individual.

Nothing and no one exists outside the Creator.

There is only One Consciousness within the totality of Creation.

The One, in Itself, is a witness.
The One, in Itself, knows everything.

Intensely profound.
Deeply wise.

O vast Creator,
O powerful Destroyer,
O loving Protector and Preserver.

Treasure of grace.
Bestower of mercy.

Bless me to be at the feet of Your sages.

Naanak this is the single love of my mind.

16-2

Fulfiller of longings.
Omnipotent Protector.

Whatever Thou does,
That is the only thing which shall be.

In the wink of an eye,
You bestow something
You take something away.

No one else knows the formula of Thy mind.

Vision of delight,
Immense happiness ever comes from Thee.

Mountains of wealth are stored in Thy home.

King among kings.
Yogi among yogis.

You purify Yourself through a disciplined practice,
And You live as a householder with total enjoyment.

Meditating and meditating,
The devoted lover becomes peaceful.

O Naanak,
The Divine Protector is beyond all limits.

16-3

This Wondrous Play of the Divine
Has no end.

All the transparent Spirits have grown weary of it.

How can a son have knowledge about the birth of his father?

The Divine One Itself strings everything on a thread.

The One bestows wisdom, meditation, and a kind nature.

Such people become servants who meditate on
The Divine Identity alone.

There are those who dwell in the three qualities,
Deluded and in doubt.

They wander through birth and death,
Coming and going.

The high and the low have their place through the One.

O Naanak, people understand this
Because the Divine imparts the understanding.

16-4

So many forms.
So many colors.

So many disguises
Made from One Love.

The expanse of Creation
Has so many shows.

The Indestructible Master
The One who manifests and merges with the Creation,

In an instant, the Divine creates
So many marvels
Present within and completely filling all places.

So many modalities
Formed with such craftsmanship.

You, Yourself measure
The worth of what You have done.

Every heart is Thine.
All places are Thine.

Naanak lives
By constantly calling upon
The Identity of the Divine.

16-5

The Divine Identity supports every being.

The Divine Identity supports the universe and its realms.

The Divine Identity supports all sacred writings.

The Divine Identity is the foundation for wisdom,
Deep listening, and meditation.

The Divine Identity holds the heavens and lower worlds in place.

The Divine Identity supports all the forms.

The Divine Identity shores up the cites of the world.

In the company of the Divine Identity,
Listen deeply with your ears
And become liberated.

By Thy kindness, people get attached
To the Identity of the Divine within them.

O Naanak,
These people dwell in the Fourth State, beyond the three qualities,
And achieve freedom.

16-6

The form is real
And the place is real.

The Supreme Being is real—
Most excellent unique One.

Real are the actions.
Real also the frequency of communication.

The True Supreme Being is merged in all.

The actions are real.
What gets created is real.

The root is real,
And real — what it produces.

The True Doer purifies
To bring out the purity.

For the person who understands this,
Everything is good.

Real is the Identity of the Creator,
Giver of comfort and peace.

The trust is real, O Naanak.
One receives it through the Sound of Wisdom.

16-7

When the sages teach, their words are true.

Through this truth,
A person enters his own heart.

If someone becomes aware enough
To assess things correctly,

He finds the state of consciousness
Where he can call upon his Divine Identity.

You, Divine One, are real.
All that You have fashioned is real.

You, Yourself, correctly know
Your own condition.

The Hand of the Creator
Moves the entire world.

No one else understands You enough
To have an opinion about it.

Nobody knows what the Creator knows.

O Naanak,
The Divine Will
Pervades everything.

16-8

These wonders of wonders
Leave me in awe.

Those who become aware find the sweetness.

The servants remain absorbed
In the colorful love of the Creator.

They acquire the treasure of the Teacher's wisdom.

They become givers
Who destroy pain and sorrow.

In their company, a person is made to swim through illusion.

By tremendous good fortune,
Someone serves these servants.

Being with them,
She becomes attuned to and absorbed in the One.

The devoted lovers sing sacred songs
About the qualities of the One who Preserves the World.

Through the blessings that come from the Sound of Wisdom,
Naanak obtains the fruit.

17

Shalok

From the Primal Beginning,
This Truth is True.

All through Time and Space,
It's True.

It is True, absolutely, now.

Naanak declares it shall be completely True forever.

17

Ashtapadi

17-1

The feet are real,
And real—the one who touches them.

The offering is real,
And real—the one who serves.

The vision is real,
And real—the one who sees it.

The Divine Identity is real—
And real the one who meditates upon it.

You, Yourself, are real,
And real—the entire Creation that You support.

You, Yourself, are the virtues
And you embody them.

The Sound Current that cuts the ego is real,
And real—what the Creator speaks.

The conscious awareness is real,
And real—the Divine appreciation that it hears.

For the realized person,
Everything is real.

Naanak is real,
And completely real is the Creator.

17-2

The one who trusts and obeys
The nature of truth within his heart,

Recognizes the Root-Source, the cause of all actions.

For the one whose heart feels confidence in the Creator,
The essence of wisdom becomes clear to her mind.

Through fear, one comes to live Beyond Fear.

That from which we originate
Is what we must merge into.

Within the substance,
The same substance gets mingled.

No one can declare them
Separate from each other.

Realizing this, the realized person develops discriminating insight.

Naanak merges in union
With the Ever-Renewing One.

17-3

The one who serves the Divine Master
Does what the command requires.

The one who serves the Divine Master
Always feels fulfilled.

The one who serves the Divine Master
Has a mind that trusts.

Pure is the way of those who serve the Divine Master.

The one who serves the Divine Master
Abides in His companionship.

The one who serves the Creator
Loves his Divine Identity.

The Creator is the Nourisher
Of His servants.

The Formless One provides protection
To the one who serves.

That person becomes a devoted servant
Who flows with the kindness of the Creator.

O Naanak,
Those who serve
Communicate with the Divine,
Breath after breath.

17-4

You, Yourself, cloak Your devotees with a veil.

You completely preserve those who serve You.

You, Yourself, bestow pre-eminence upon Your servants.

You cause those who serve you
To repeatedly call upon their Divine Identity.

You, Yourself, protect the honor of those who serve You.

No one can accurately measure the extent of Your Being.

No one equals the status of one who serves the Creator.

The one who serves the Creator
Is the most exalted of all.

Whoever the Creator, Itself, assigns to do Its service,

Naanak, that servant manifests her radiance in the ten directions.

17-5

Should the Divine infuse Its power into the tiniest insect,

Then an army of millions
Would get turned into ash.

Should the breath, itself, cease to be drawn,
The Divine hand could still extend Its protection.

The human being makes many kinds of efforts,
Yet these actions only create anxiety and pain.

There is no one else who is
The Destroyer or the Protector.

The Divine completely guards
All of the creatures.

O Being of Breath—
Why do you ponder?

Naanak calls upon the Master—
Invisible and wonderful.

17-6

Over and over and over again,
Call upon the Creator.

Drink in the awareness of your own Deathlessness.
It will satisfy your mind and body.

The one who flows with the Sound of Wisdom,
Obtains the priceless jewel of his Divine Identity.

Such a person sees nothing but the One.

The treasure of the Divine Identity
Is when It expresses Itself through color and form.

The Divine Identity brings peace.
Keep company with your Divinely-given Self.

The nectar-taste of his Divine Identity
Fulfills the man.

Through the Divine Identity,
A person's mind and body merges with his own Divine Identity.

Remain present with your Divine Identity,
Whether standing, sitting or sleeping.

Naanak says—the servant performs this task forever.

17-7

O tongue, day and night,
Express your appreciation.

The Creator gives this gift to His servants.

When the Devoted Lover does it,
The soul becomes delighted and happy.

The Devoted Lover remains merged with the Creative Lord.

Such a person knows
All that was
And all that shall be.

She recognizes the Divine Plan of the Creator.

Who can describe it—the grandeur of the One?

I cannot know even one of Thy virtues.

Throughout the eight watches of the day,
Dwell in the Creator's presence.

Says Nanak, the people who do this
Become complete.

17-8

O my mind, take shelter with the spiritual people.

Give your mind and body
To those who serve the Divine.

The person who, within himself,
Has recognized the Creator
Can bestow all things.

Come under the protection of such a one—
You will obtain all comfort and peace.

Upon seeing a truly spiritual person,
All the pain, mistakes, and errors of the past disappear.

Leave behind all other wisdom.

Become attached to serving those who serve.

Your comings and goings
Shall happen no more.

O Naanak, make an offering of yourself forever
To the feet of someone like this.

18
Shalok

The True Protector
Has knowledge of his Divine Identity
Through the Sound of Wisdom that guides him to truth.

Naanak, in his company,
Those who seek wisdom sing about the Divine,
And become liberated.

18

Ashtapadi

18-1

The Sound of Wisdom that leads to Truth
Nurtures and protects those who seek.

The Teacher has compassion, forever,
Towards those who do His service.

The Sound of Wisdom takes away
The subconscious dirt and foolish understanding
Of those who seek.

The sayings of the Teacher allow a person
To give voice to the Essence of her Divine Identity.

The Sound of Wisdom that leads to Truth
Cuts the shackles of those who seek.

Those who seek, withdraw from vice and wrong action
Through the Sound of Wisdom.

The Teacher of Truth
Gives the treasure of the Divine Identity.

Those who seek Truth through the Sound of Wisdom
Are extremely fortunate.

The Teacher of Truth adjusts the affairs of those who seek
In this world and the next.

O Naanak, the Sound of Wisdom that leads to Truth
Protects the souls of those who seek.

18-2

The trusted servant who lives in the Teacher's home
Mentally endures the Teacher's command.

He performs the assigned task,
Knowing nothing.

Within his heart, he meditates always
On the continual Presence
Of the Divine Essence
Within his Identity.

He has sold his mind to the Teacher of Truth,
Who possesses it,
And corrects the servant's deeds.

The servant performs the service desirelessly,
And by so doing, acquires the Master.

O Divine One,
By Your kindness, You, Yourself,
Do these things.

Naanak, such a servant understands the Teacher's wisdom.

18-3

When the mind completely surrenders in obedience to the Teacher,
Then that servant knows the reality of the All-Powerful, Pervading One.

The Teacher of Truth holds the essence
Of the Divine Identity within Its heart.

Let me surrender myself, time and again
As a sacrifice to the One
Who takes us from darkness to light.

All the treasures are given to the soul.

Throughout the day and night,
Steep yourself in the love
Of the Vast, All-Powerful Creator.

The servant is inside the Creator,
And the Vast, All-Powerful Creator is within the servant.

They exist in that Oneness.
Have no doubt about it.

She attains thousands of wisdoms,
Which never depart.

Naanak, through this method,
Blessed by fortune,
A person attains the One who can take her from darkness to light.

18-4

Looking upon those who live in the Purity of their Spirits
Is a fruitful vision.

Touch their feet and become empty—
You will purify yourself.

Become part of their community,
And enjoy the virtues of the One
Who created the sun and the moon.

Sing in the royal court
Of the Vast, All-Powerful Creator.

Deeply listening to the words of such people,
The ears become satisfied.

The mind becomes content,
And the soul merges with Her Husband.

The Sound of Wisdom is completely perfect.
The mantra never fades away.

People become sacred
When they behold their own Immortal Nature.

Their virtues have no limit.
No one can calculate their value.

Naanak,
Whoever pleases You, Divine One,
Is brought into union with Thee.

18-5

Let my tongue praise the One
Numerous times.

The Divine Protector of Truth
Has perfect discriminating awareness.

The beings, who live by breath,
Do not have the capacity
To speak about this at all.

Our senses cannot perceive the Creator,
Who exists far beyond our reach
And who dwells in the consciousness of Ultimate Freedom.

Beyond Sustenance.
Beyond Vengeance.
Bestower of contentment and peace.

No one can evaluate
The worth of the One.

Many Devoted Lovers
Endlessly acknowledge the Divine.

Within their hearts, they focus upon
The Lotus Feet of the Creator.

May I forever give myself, without condition,
To the Sound of Wisdom that guides me to Truth.

O Naanak,
When the gift of grace comes to a person,
Then she repeatedly calls upon the Divine.

18-6

There are some people who acquire this taste of the Divine Reality.

When they drink in the memory of their own Deathlessness,
Then they achieve immortality.

Such a man shall never get destroyed.

His mind manifests the Divine qualities.

Every hour of the day,
He experiences the Divine Reality in his own Identity.

He gives instructions about the Ultimate Reality to those who serve.

Even though he may keep company with the creation
And its enticements,
He does not become degraded by the experience.

The One continual presence
Of the Divine Essence
Protects his mind.

He burns bright as a lantern
In the blinding dark.

O Naanak,
Through such people,
Delusions, attachments and suffering
Get destroyed.

18-7

In the midst of the burning fire,
A cool tranquility prevails.

O Brother,
There is a bliss that happens when your actions
Reflect the reality of your soul.
Suffering and pain become a temporary experience.

Anxiety about life and death
Disappear.

This happens through the perfect instructions
Given by people of wisdom.

Fear ends,
And one dwells Beyond Fear.

All the diseases of the mind get destroyed.

This comes to those, upon whom,
The kindness of the Divine
Continuously flows.

In the company of those who live by purity, discipline, and grace,
Call upon the Identity of the One who Destroys the Demons
And Protects the World.

The days of wandering in doubt,
Through many existences,
Have ended.

O Naanak,
Listen deeply with your ears
To the praises of the Divine.

18-8

Divine One,
You exist Beyond Form,
And You dwell in the Manifested Creation,
As well.

Your incredible artistry supports the Universe,
Charming and enchanting all the Beings.

You, Yourself, feel wonder-struck
At what You have made,
Divine Master.

Only You can experience Your own worth.

There is no other power
Except the Divine Reality.

The One exists in absolute presence—
Dwelling within and filling all things.

You contemplate, in enjoyment,
These treasures of form and color.

In the company of the wise and disciplined people,
This awareness blossoms.

You, Yourself, fashion the creation
Continuously throughout time.

Over and over again,
Naanak sacrifices himself to Thee.

19

Shalok

Nothing goes with you in the end,
Except for the sacred songs you sing.
Poison turns everything else to dust.

Work hard and earn the experience of the Divine,
Ever-present within your Identity.

Naanak, this is the essence of wealth.

19

Ashtapadi

19-1

Meeting with the spiritual elders,
You will gain insight and understanding.

Focus your thoughts
Directly on the One,
And let your Divine Identity support you.

Friend—forget about all other solutions.

Place the Lotus Feet of the Divine
Within the heart of your very heart.

Such is the Power of the Creator,
Who is the cause behind all actions.

Hold tightly to the creativity of the Divine within your Identity.

By incredible fortune,
You accumulate this treasure.

The spiritual elders share their pure advice.
Protect your mind
By placing your hopes in the One.

Naanak,
Then all sickness
Will cease to exist.

19-2

You wake up and chase after wealth
To the ends of the earth.

Yet, you will acquire the same wealth
By serving the Divine Reality in all things.

You constantly long for peace, my friend.

Love the community of people who live by grace and discipline.
There, you will find peace.

You do great deeds
To build your honor and reputation.

Yet, that beautiful honor comes from worshiping the Divine
And taking sanctuary with It.

The illness will not leave
Despite so many remedies.

Let the medicine of the Divine Reality
Melt away your sickness.

Among all treasures,
Your Creative Divine Identity
Is *the* treasure.

Keep repeating this, Naanak.
You shall be embraced
In the Royal Court of the One.

19-3

The experience of the Divine Reality within one's Identity
Awakens the mind.

After running in ten different directions,
The mind comes to a still place.

No obstacles attach themselves to it.

For the person within whose heart
The Divine Reality makes Its home,

He experiences the Creative Power within his Identity,
And can face a fiery death.

Creating a continuous communication
Between the Infinite Spirit and the self-in-time-and-space
Brings an everlasting peace.

Fear is destroyed,
And all hopes get completed.

Becoming a devoted lover of the Divine,
The soul-self lights up.

In this manner, people leave their homes,
And dwell with the Indestructible One.

Says Naanak, this is how the noose of death gets cut.

19-4

The person who lives according to truth
Talks about the Essence as she understands it.

Those who experience birth and death
Are raw and immature.

By serving the Creator,
Comings and goings cease.

Abandon everything else,
And take shelter in the ever-present guidance of the Teachings.

This shall save the jewel of your life.

With the breath as your support,
Meditate on *Har...Har*
The Sound of the Divine in the beat of your heart.

There are so many remedies,
Yet, still, one does not find freedom,
Even by understanding all sacred writings.

Let your mind remain focused
On the devoted love of the Divine.

Naanak, then the mind shall receive
The fruit of its longing.

19-5

Your wealth will not keep you company when you depart.
Why do you cling to it, foolish mind?

Your children, friends, family and spouse—
Who among them
Will bring you to the Master?

Your kingdom expands
Into the colorful play of Creation.

Yet, within that territory, what can free you?

Horses, elephants, and riding in chariots—
This display is fake,
And fake—the vastness of it.

In your ignorance,
You don't understand
That the One gives to you.

O Naanak, regret happens
When you forget the Divine Identity.

19-6

Take the Guru's advice, O Innocent One—

Without devotion, many wise people have drowned.

O friend, with your mind,
Love the Divine Reality.

This will purify your awareness.

Place the lotus feet of the Master in your mind.

Then, the burden of the mistakes you have made,
Lifetime after lifetime, shall depart.

Repeatedly call upon your Divine Identity,
And get others to call upon their Divine Identity as well.

You will become liberated
By deeply listening,
Talking about it
And holding to the discipline.

Understand this elemental truth—
The Divine Identity exists in the Essence of Creation.

Naanak sings about the virtues of the One
With intuitive ease and pleasure.

19-7

Singing about Your virtues,
A person crosses over the muck.

The poisonous actions that come from ego
Get destroyed.

One becomes carefree
And dwells in peace.

Focus on the breath,
And remember the Creativity of your Divine Identity.

Abandon all the clever games of the mind.

In the community of those who live by purity and grace,
You shall obtain the wealth of Truth.

Become the merchant
Who accumulates the capital of the Divine Reality.

You will find peace here,
And you shall receive honor
In the Divine Court.

Behold the One within everything.

Says Naanak, this shall happen for those
Upon whose forehead it has been written.

19-8

Call upon the One.
Appreciate the One.

Establish a dialogue with the One.
Let the One come in your mind.

Sing about the qualities
Of the endless and only One

With your body and mind,
Repeatedly call upon
The One Supreme Lover.

The Divine Reality, Itself,
Is One
Within Its Own Oneness.

The Master abides within,
Filling everything completely,
And is the cause of all that happens.

The One takes part
In countless shows.

Worshipping the One,
All your mistakes and transgressions
Leave.

Those who, from within,
Have given their minds and bodies totally
To the One Creator,

Shall come to know the One,
O Naanak,
Through the gift of the Teachings.

20
Shalok

O Creator,
After traveling and wandering for so long,
I have fallen under Your protection.

Naanak makes this request.
Master, please focus my attention on Thee.

20

Ashtapadi

20-1

I am a beggar, O Master,
Who begs for these gifts.

Let Your kindness prevail.
Bestow upon me
The Divine Reality within my Identity.

I seek the dust
Of the spiritually-wise people
Who serve You.

O Great Creator,
Let my trust become perfect.

May I always and forever
Sacredly sing
About Your virtues, O Master.

Breath after breath,
I meditate on You alone,
Divine One.

With love, let me attach myself
To Your Lotus Feet.

In every moment,
May I be the devoted lover
Of my Master,

Who is my only Protection
And my only Support.

Naanak begs to experience
The Identity of the Creator.

20-2

Directly perceiving the Creator,
One becomes profoundly peaceful.

Some rare person receives the taste of the Divine Reality.

Those who enjoy this taste are satisfied.

The man who knows he is complete
Never fluctuates.

Absolutely filled with love,
The nectar permeates through him.

In the company of the spiritually-wise people,
His happiness grows.

He detaches himself from everything,
Except the shelter of the Beyond.

From within, a light shines,
Night and day, attuned with love.

By profound fortune,
He repeatedly calls upon the Creator.

Naanak, one becomes content
By getting absorbed in the Divine Identity.

20-3

Whatever the trusted servant longs for gets fulfilled.

Through the Sound of Wisdom that leads to truth,
One's intellect becomes crystal clear.

When the Creator shows kindness to His servant,
That trusted servant feels ecstasy always.

The bonds are cut.
The student is free.

Birth, death,
Suffering and illusion
Get destroyed.

All hopes, virtues,
And acts of faith
Are completed.

He abides delightfully
In the continuous presence of the Divine Master.

Whoever belongs to Thee
Gets united with Thee.

Naanak, through devotion,
One merges with the Divine Identity.

20-4

Why forget the One,
Who does not deny anyone's efforts?

Why forget the One
Who knows what you have done?

Why forget the One
Who gives absolutely everything?

Why forget the One
Who is the life of every creature?

Why forget the One
Who protects You in the fire?

Through the gift of the Sound of Wisdom,
Some rare person realizes this.

Why forget the One
Who draws the poison from you—

Who breaks through the cycle of rebirth?

The perfect Teacher gives me
The understanding of the Essence of Truth.

Servant Naanak meditates
On the Creator, alone.

20-5

O Beloved people of purity,
Do this work.

Detach yourself from everything else,
And repeatedly call upon
The creativity of your Divine Identity.

Create a continuous dialogue
Between your Infinite Spirit and the self-in-time-and-space.
Then you will find peace.

Call upon your Divine Identity,
And help others call upon their Divine Identity, as well.

Love and devotion
Will cause you to swim across the illusions of the world.

Without devotion, the body becomes dust.

The Divine Identity contains
All happiness, comforts, and treasures.

Even those who are drowning receive rest.

All sufferings and illness get destroyed,

O Naanak,
When you call upon your Divine Identity,
The treasure of virtues.

20-6

Let love and affection grow.
Drink in the taste of it.

This will create a sweet satisfaction
Within the mind and body.

Peace and happiness come
When the eyes perceive the Immortal One.

Washing the feet of those who live by discipline and grace,
The mind blossoms.

The mind and body of the devoted servant
Become dyed in the color of love.

Rare are the people
Who keep company with them.

Out of compassion,
The Creator gives this one blessing.

Through the grace of the Sound of Wisdom,
We become attached to our Divine Identity.

There is no way to fully express
Our praise and appreciation of Thee.

O Naanak,
The Divine remains merged
With everything.

20-7

The Forgiving Creator, kind to the poor,

Is forever gracious and loving
To those who are devoted.

The One who Preserves and Sustains the World
Oversees the affairs of the helpless.

That One protects and nurtures
Every heart.

The Primal Lord
Is the Cause and the Doer.

He is the breath and support
Of his adoring servants.

Whoever repeatedly calls upon the One
Will surely become pure.

The devoted person loves.
Her psyche vibrates with love.

We are lowly, ignorant creatures,
Empty of virtue.

Naanak takes refuge in Your shelter,
O Great Divine Protector.

20-8

You can access all the etheric realms,
Find liberation and freedom,

By singing about the virtues of the Divine
For even just a moment.

So many royal territories
Dawn and grow,

When the mind talks about
The Divine Reality within every Identity.

So much food,
So many clothes and companions come

When the tongue continually repeats,
"Har...Har..."
The Sound of the Divine in the beat of the heart.

The actions become superior,
The person —radiant and prosperous

When the *Gurmantra* lives
Complete in the heart.

When the Creator gives you a home
In the community of those who live by discipline and grace,

Then, O Nanaak,
A peaceful happiness
Lights up everything.

21

Shalok

The Formless One,
In the zero state,
Deeply meditates upon Itself
As both manifest and unmanifest.

The One creates, O Naanak,
And the One wanders through lifetimes,
Repeatedly calling upon Itself.

21

Ashtapadi

21-1

When no perceivable form existed,

Then how could someone act virtuously,
Or get lost in the darkness of his mistakes?

When the One Itself
Focused on the zero point and meditated deeply,

Then how could communities become hostile,
And engage in opposition?

When no symbol could be spoken,
Describing the Divine One,

Then who felt joy and who felt sorrow?

When the Vast, All-Powerful Creator
Dwelt within the Self of Its very Self,

Then who experienced attachment?
Who doubted, in illusion?

You, Yourself, play,
And You have infused Yourself everywhere.

Naanak, there is nobody
Except the One Doer.

21-2

When the Creator meditated all on Its own,

Then who got released from his bonds,
And who kept the account?

When the One Divine Presence existed,
Inaccessible and limitless,

Then who took birth in heaven or hell?

When the Unmanifested Awareness
Enjoyed Its own deep state of ease,

Then where did the creative polarity
Of Sacred Masculine and Sacred Feminine reside?

When the Immortal Light focused
On Its own Self, within Itself,

Then who became fearless,
And who felt afraid?

You, Yourself, are the One who creates Your own marvels.

O Naanak, the Great Master
Is beyond our perception,
And beyond any boundary.

21-3

When the Indestructible One
Maintained Its posture of peace,

Then how could the cycle of birth and death be destroyed?

When the Creator presided,
Absolutely complete,

Then who feared the messenger of death?

When the One Divine Master existed—
Imperishable and beyond perception,

Then which angels asked the questions,
And who wrote the secret record?

When the Master, in Its far-reaching depth,
Dwelt pure and beyond perception,

Then who got liberated?
And who was tied down with obstacles?

You, within Your own Self,
Are incredibly astounding.

O Naanak,
You are the One
Who creates Your own form.

21-4

When the Honorable Protector presided,
Crystal clear in His Being,

Then no dirt existed,
So what could get cleansed?

When the Formless One dwelt pure,
In absolute freedom,

Then who lived in honor?
Who in self-centered pride?

When the Great Cosmic Master
Was the only Divine Form,

Then who practiced deceit and attachment to vice?

When the form of Divine Light
Merged into the company of Its own radiance,

Then who became hungry,
And who felt satisfied?

One Doer alone
Does all the deeds.

O Naanak, there is no way to account for what
The Creator performs.

21-5

When the Divine One kept company with Its own splendor,

Then who became a mother or father,
A friend, child, or sibling?

When the One, Itself, was the expert
Of all arts and skills,

Then who needed to understand
Any sacred teaching?

When the Divine One, within the Self of Its very Self,
Focused on Its heart,

Then where did people discuss
Good omens and bad portents?

When the One held Itself in a high state of consciousness,
While also remaining close to Its Being,

Then who was a Master?
And who called anyone a student?

Amazingly amazing,
Dwelling in awe.

Naanak,
You, Divine One, know Your condition alone.

21-6

When the One, who is never betrayed,
Always unified,
And undifferentiated in Its aspect,
Remained merged with Itself,

In that consciousness—
Who could the Creative Illusion ensnare?

When the One, who touches no other,
Bowed to Itself,

There, the three qualities had no way to enter.

When the One and only Noble One,
Abided within Its own Oneness,

Then who lived carefree?
Who became anxious or worried?

When the Divine, in Its own Self,
Presided as Master,

Then who spoke about sacred matters,
And who was the listener?

So very Infinite,
The highest of the high,

O Naanak,
You alone reach Yourself.

21-7

When You, Yourself, fashioned the form of the world,
With all of its pleasures,

You did so by expanding
Through the three qualities.

Then people discussed their errors and virtues.

Some wished for hell,
And some wanted heaven.

This world burns,
Entangled in the Creative Illusion.

Ego, doubt, fear, and fate.

Torment and peace.
Honor and dishonor.

So many methods get described.

You, Yourself, observe Your own play.

Naanak,
When the play folds back in on itself,
Then all will be One.

21-8

Wherever the Unconditional Divine One dwells,
There you will find people of devotion.

Wherever the Creative Consciousness expands,
That expansion brings honor to the wise and the pure.

You are the Blessed Master of both aspects.

And You have made those aspects radiant.

You fashion this wonderful miracle,
And blissfully make sport with it.

With a neutral awareness,
You enjoy the sweet taste of it.

By Thy pleasure,
You attach someone to his own Divine Identity.

By Thy pleasure,
You cause someone to play in the game.

You are innumerable, unfathomable, incalculable, and unparalleled.

Darling One,
As You move me to speak,
That is how servant Naanak speaks.

22

Shalok

O Master of all,
You are the Doer within the life of every being.

Naanak, the One Consciousness expands Itself through form.
Who else is there to perceive?

22

Ashtapadi

22-1

You, Yourself, talk about sacred subjects,
And You are the one who listens.

You remain One within Yourself,
And You manifest the show.

You created the world for Your own pleasure,

And when Your Divine Will decides it,
Everything will merge back into You.

Nothing happens except what comes through You,
In Your originality.

You, Yourself, are the thread
That strings the entire Universe together.

Creator—because of You someone understands this.

That servant of Yours receives the experience
Of his Ultimate Identity.

He knows the essence of reality,
And perceives everything impartially.

Naanak, such a one understands the entire universe.

22-2

All the creatures are like musical instruments
In the hands of the Creator.

Compassionate to the poor.
Master of the desolate.

Those who the One protects shall never be destroyed.

If the Divine, in Its mind, forgets about someone,
Then that person dies.

If someone abandons the Creator,
Who else can he turn to?

There is just One King,
Pure and unattached,
Who presides as the head of all.

The Creator's hand guides the path of every living being.

Know that the One keeps you company,
Within and without.

The Creator is an Infinite, boundless treasure of virtues.

Slave Naanak surrenders himself as a sacrifice to Thee, forever.

22-3

The Omniscient One, through compassion,
Completes everything.

Overseeing all the beings,
The Creator acts with kindness.

The One moves skillfully,
And Itself knows the reason why.

The Inner-Knower of the heart
Abides, diffused, within.

The One has so many methods to guard Its creatures.

Whoever the Creator has fashioned meditates on Him.

As it pleases Thee,
Someone merges with the Divine.

Those who love the Divine
Sing about Its virtues.

Within their minds, they practice trust
And surrender to the command.

Naanak, recognize the One
As the Doer of all the deeds.

22-4

For the person who becomes attached to the One Creative Identity,
Her hopes do not go unfulfilled.

She performs the service that she is called to do.

By deeply understanding the Divine Will,
She attains the supreme state of consciousness.

From this elevated state,
No discussion is required.

The Formless One dwells within her mind.

Her bonds break and she lives beyond vengeance.

Day and night, adore the feet
Of those Teachings that take you
From darkness to light.

Then you will experience peace in this world,
And happiness in the next.

O Naanak, such people merge with the Creator, Itself.

22-5

You become blissful
By joining the community of those who live by purity and grace.

Singing about the qualities of the Creator,
You reach the peak of ecstasy.

Reflect on the essence of the One,
Whose Identity formed the sun and the moon.

Then you will become liberated through this
Rare and precious human body.

Sing about the virtues of the Divine
With immortal language.

Your breath will carry you across the ocean of life.
You will merge into the Light.

Look—twenty-four hours a day
The Creator stays close to you.

Let the One erase your ignorance
And destroy the darkness.

Listen to the teachings,
And let them dwell in your heart.

Then, Naanak, you will receive the fruits
That your mind desires.

22-6

All of your affairs in this world and the next
Will be arranged for you,

When you focus, in your heart,
On the One whose Identity formed the sun and the moon.

The perfect Teacher has imparted the perfect instructions.

The mind that lives by these instructions can determine what is true.

With mind and body,
Call upon your Divine Identity
And attune yourself with love to it.

All suffering, afflictions, and mental fears will disappear.

Trade in the business of the Ultimate Reality.

In the Divine Court,
Your account shall be settled.

Within your mind,
Let the One support and protect you.

Naanak, then you shall come and go no more.

22-7

How can someone become distant from the Divine?

Meditating on the Sustainer
Grants a person freedom.

By calling upon the Fearless One,
All one's fears cease to exist.

The being of breath gets released
Through the kindness of the Creator.

Those whom the Creator protects never suffer.

The mind becomes happy and peaceful
When it calls upon its Divine Identity.

Worries leave,
And the ego—the false sense of self—
Is destroyed.

Nothing rivals the person who lives like this.

When the great sun, the Sound of Wisdom,
Takes Its place above someone's head,

Then, Naanak,
Her work becomes complete.

22-8

When the intelligence is perfected in wisdom,
Then one's perception becomes immortal.

Seeing with this sight,
A person gets liberated from the world.

Nothing compares to the Lotus Feet of the Divine.

Fruitful is the vision of the beautiful form that the Creator takes.

Blessed the service.
Approved the servant.

The one who knows the Inner-Reality of every heart
Is chief among men.

Whoever's mind dwells in this consciousness
Flourishes with happiness.

Death does not come close to him.

He becomes immortal,
And achieves the status of immortality.

O Naanak,
Meditate upon the Divine
In the community of those who live
By purity, discipline, and grace.

23
Shalok

The Guide of Light bestows the balm of wisdom,
Which destroys ignorance and darkness.

O Naanak,
Through the kindness of the Divine,
The mind becomes enlightened
When it meets a realized soul.

23
Ashtapadi
23-1

In the company of those who live
By purity, grace, and discipline,
People perceive the Creator within themselves,

And become attached to the sweetness of the Creator's Identity.

All material reality exists
In the home of the Sovereign One.

So many colors,
So many varied sites to see.

The nine treasures, and the awareness of one's own deathlessness
Come from the Identity of the Creator,

Which rests within the human form.

Deeply meditating,
Absorbed in the experience of nothingness,
The Soundless Cosmic Vibration resounds.

There is no way to discuss
How marvelously wonderful this is.

Only those to whom the Divine reveals it
Can see it.

Naanak, such a person has a vast and perceptive awareness.

23-2

The inner world and the outer reality
Have no limits.

The Divine, Adorable One
Resides, present, within each heart.

On the earth,
A person can find both heaven and hell.

All the experiences in existence
Are wholly nurtured and protected.

The Vast, All-Powerful Creator is one with the forces of nature—
Its grasses, forests, and mountains.

As it is ordered, so it is done.

In the air, water, and fire,

Pervading across the four quarters and the ten directions.

No place remains separate from that Consciousness.

O Naanak,
Through the kindness of the Sound of Wisdom,
Peace prevails within me.

23-3

See the One in the sacred writings of different faiths.

The One also dwells in the moon and the stars.

The vibration of the Creator exists
In everything that gets spoken.

You, Yourself, are steady and unshakeable.
It is not possible to move You.

You playfully play with complete artistry and skill.

Your quality is priceless.
No one can assess Your worth.

Your Light abides within all Lights.

The Divine Master is the warp and woof
That maintains everything in its place.

When the grace of the Teachings destroys delusion and doubt,

Then, Naanak,
People place their trust in the One.

23-4

The spiritually wise servants
See the Creator Lord in everything.

In the heart of the spiritually-wise servants,
Only Cosmic Law exists.

The spiritually-wise servants
Listen to nothing but positive words.

They keep company with the One who made the sun and the moon,
Whose presence fills the entire Creation.

Here is the method
For those who live a superior life.

The spiritually awake people
Speak only words of Truth.

Whatever happens, they accept it
With peace and ease,

Knowing that the Divine Master
Causes all the deeds to be done.

The One lives both within and without.

O Naanak,
This Divine vision that I see
Completely fascinates me.

23-5

The One, Itself, is authentic and true,
And all that It does is authentic and true.

The entire Creation manifests through the Creator.

The Divine acts according to Its own pleasure.

The One Consciousness vibrates through form
According to Its own Will.

It has so many powers that we don't understand.

As it pleases You, You cause someone to merge with Thee.

Who is close to you?
And who far away?

You within the Self of Your very Self
Fill everything with Your presence,

And You cause someone to realize her Inner State.

Naanak, the Divine gives this understanding
To those who serve.

23-6

You put all the elements to good use,
And You are the Observer within every eye.
All the material forms make up Your body.
You praise Yourself, and You also listen.

The One has fashioned this place of coming and going.

The Created Reality moves according to the Divine Command.

You dwell in the midst of it all—untouched.

Whatever someone says,
That is You speaking.

According to Your order, we come.
According to Your order, we go.

Naanak, merger with Thee happens
By Thy Will alone.

23-7

This is how things happen
So nothing is bad.

How can anyone else do anything?

The Superior One acts in a very positive manner.

The Divine, within Itself, knows why.

Dwelling in the Ultimate Reality,
The Creator supports the Truth in everything.

The One is the warp and woof,
Intermingling with the community of life.

No one can accurately measure or express
The Creator's condition.

If some Equal Consciousness came along,
Only It could understand.

All that the Creator does is approved.

O Naanak, this knowledge comes as a blessing,
Through the Sound of Wisdom that guides us to Light.

23-8

Whoever has this knowledge always lives in peace.

The Creator, Itself, embraces in union such a person.

He becomes wealthy, establishes a good family, and enjoys honor.

His heart holds the Venerable Divine One,
So he becomes liberated while alive.

Blessed, blessed, most fortunately blessed
Is the coming of such a person.

The grace that prevails in his life
Causes the entire world to swim across the ocean of existence.

The human being has come to experience this taste—

And in the company of others,
Her Divine Identity will enter into her awareness.

Free and liberated herself,
She liberates the world.

Naanak forever salutes and bows to such a soul as this.

24

Shalok

Focus your attention on the completely perfect Creator
Whose Identity is perfectly complete.

Naanak attains complete perfection
By singing about the qualities
Of the Perfect One.

24

Ashtapadi

24-1

Listening deeply to the instructions
Of the completely perfect Teacher,

You will perceive the Vast Omnipotent Creator close by.

In every breath, establish a dialogue
With the Sustainer of the Universe.

Then you shall cross over
The anxiety in your mind.

Abandon the impulses of your temporary desires.

Let the mind beg for the dust of the spiritually disciplined people.

Leave your ego behind
And make this request.

That the company of those who live
By purity, grace, and discipline
Will carry you across
This ocean of fire.

Fill your treasury with the wealth
Of the Divine Reality.

Naanak bows to and salutes
The Sound of Wisdom, which is perfectly complete.

24-2

Liberation, happiness, ease, and delight

Will come when you honorably worship
The Endlessly Blissful One
In the company of those who live
By purity, grace, and discipline.

Darling, you become liberated by this,
And the hell of your life gets removed.

Through the qualities of the Universal Sustainer,
Drink in the taste of your own Deathlessness.

Reflect, in your awareness, on the Cosmic Nurturer.

One form displaying a vast array of colors.

The One who holds the Universe in Its navel
Shows kindness to the down-trodden.

Destroyer of suffering,
Completely perfect in compassion.

Align yourself and constantly communicate
With your Divine Identity.

O Naanak,
This is what supports my being.

24-3

The wise people speak
The highest spiritual poetry.

These beloved jewels are beyond any price.

Deeply listening to their words,
A person earns her liberation.

She liberates the world, as well,
Helping it swim across.

Such a life is successful,
And the companions of such a one
Also find success.

Her mind remains attached to and dyed with
The Divine Reality.

The Soundless Cosmic Vibration of the Shabad plays for her.

Deeply listening, she hears the roaring thunder of the Creator
And feels bliss.

The Vastly Honorable Divine Sustainer
Manifests upon her forehead.

O Naanak, those who remain in her company
Get saved, as well.

24-4

Honoring that the Divine has offered Its protection,
We have come under Its shelter.

By His kindness,
The Creator has caused our union with Him.

Hostility ceases to exist,
And we become the dust of all.

We experience our Divine Immortal Identity
In the company of those who live
By discipline, purity, and grace.

Delight happens through the Invisible Touch of the Teacher.

We perfect ourselves,
Serving the Divine's servants,

Which shields us from the sickness
Of our daily troubles and cares.

We listen to the Name of the One
Who formed the sun and the moon,
And speak it with our tongues.

The Creator flows with compassion,
And that is His grace.

O Naanak, our merchandise has successfully completed its journey.

24-5

O my sacred friends,
Appreciate the Creator,

With concentrated awareness
And careful attention.

This spiritual song of *Sukhmani*
Effortlessly expresses
The Identity of the One who Sustains the Universe
And Its virtues.

Whoever's mind dwells with this song
Becomes the treasure, himself

All his wishes get completed.

He becomes known as the highest respected leader
In all the worlds,

And obtains the most exalted status.

Then, he never comes and goes again.

Such a servant leaves this life,
Having earned the wealth of the Divine Reality.

O Naanak, this happens for those
To whom it is given.

24-6

Living blissfully—beyond attachment,
Tranquility, subtle powers,
And the nine treasures,

Enlightened understanding,
Wisdom, and all supernatural faculties,

Learning, inner purification,
Yoga, and meditations on the Divine Master,

Superior wisdom, and the most excellent healing bath,

The four blessings, and the unfolding of the lotus,

Abiding in the midst of life
With total unattachment,

Beauty, cleverness, and the knower of the Essence,

Holding the One in your vision
With impartial perception,

These fruits come to the servant, O Naanak,
Who speaks with her mouth

And who listens, with her mind,
To the Teacher's explanation of the Divine Identity.

24-7

Whoever, in their minds, meditates repeatedly on this treasure,

Becomes elevated in their consciousness,
Within every age.

The Identity of the One who Sustains the Universe,
And Its virtues,
Exists in the sound of this Divine frequency.

The sacred scriptures describe it.

All theological doctrines refer
To the Identity of the One Divine Reality.

Those who love the Sustainer of the Universe
Have relaxed and restful minds.

Millions of faults get erased in the community of those
Who live by purity, grace, and discipline.

Through the kindness of spiritual people,
A person escapes the experience of death.

Those foreheads upon which the Creator has placed Its grace,

O Naanak, come under the protection
Of the pure, disciplined ones.

24-8

Whoever's mind dwells on these words,
And who listens to them with love,

Comes to understand
The Creator and the Divine Reality,

The suffering of birth and death gets taken away.

This rare and special human body
Instantly becomes liberated.

Such a person lives purely,
With a radiant beauty,
And communicates from the frequency of his Immortality.

He merges with the Identity of the One
Within his mind.

Pain, sickness, fear, and delusion
Are destroyed.

Her identity becomes that of a sage.
Her actions reflect her purity,

And her reputation becomes the most exalted of all.

Naanak, because of these virtues,
The name of this song is *Sukhmani*—
That which crystallizes the mind
Into the jewel of peace.

Who is Siri Singh Sahib Bhai Sahib Harbhajan Singh KhalsaYogiji?

In 1969, Harbhajan Singh Khalsa Yogiji (Yogi Bhajan) came to the United States to teach Sikh values and Kundalini Yoga. Through his inspiration, hundreds of thousands of people in the West have heard the teachings of the Sikh Gurus and have embraced the Sikh path. To learn about him and his teachings on Sikh Dharma, visit www.sikhdharma.org.

Who is Ek Ong Kaar Kaur Khalsa?

Ek Ong Kaar Kaur Khalsa is a Western-born woman who, after a long spiritual search, adopted the Sikh path. She is a writer who lives in New Mexico and currently works as the Program Manager for SikhNet.com.

To order additional copies of *Sukhmani Sahib* by Guru Arjan—poetically interpreted by Ek Ong Kaar Kaur Khalsa—visit: www.a-healing.com or www.ekongkaark.com.

To learn more about Sikh Dharma, Kundalini Yoga and the Teachings of Yogi Bhajan, visit:

www.3HO.org
www.a-healing.com
www.KRIteachings.org
www.libraryofteachings.com
www.sikhdharma.org
www.sikhnet.com
www.spiritvoyage.com

CPSIA information can be obtained
at www.ICGtesting.com
Printed in the USA
FSOW03n0826290317
32450FS